# WAYS TO IMPROVE YOUR
# POWERBOAT DRIVING

G000075083

Published by Adlard Coles Nautical
an imprint of A & C Black Publishers Ltd
38 Soho Square, London, W1D 3HB
www.adlardcoles.com

First edition 2008

ISBN 978-0-7136-8269-4

A CIP catalogue record for this book is
available from the British Library.

This book is produced using paper that is
made from wood grown in managed,
sustainable forests. It is natural, renewable
and recyclable. The logging and
manufacturing processes conform to the
environmental regulations of the country of
origin.

Typeset in 9pt MetaPlusNormal
Printed and bound in China by Wing King Tong

Note: while all reasonable care has been
taken in the publication of this book, the
publisher takes no responsibility for the use
of the methods or products described in the
book.

# 50

## WAYS TO
## IMPROVE
## YOUR
## **POWERBOAT**
## **DRIVING**

## DAG PIKE

ADLARD COLES NAUTICAL
LONDON

# contents

## THE BASICS

## FAST BOAT DESIGN

## UNDERSTANDING YOUR BOAT

## THE PRIMARY CONTROLS

# contents

Driving a displacement boat at leisurely speeds leaves you all the time in the world to make decisions – not that there are too many decisions to make at single digit speeds, because you will just tend to set a comfortable speed and go. That all changes when the boat is planing and you are travelling at speeds of 30 knots or more. The first thing you have to appreciate is that the time available for reacting to situations becomes compressed as the speed rises and this means that a much more intense focus is needed for driving the boat.

The speed factor affects different aspects of the driving experience. For example, when you're driving the boat at higher speeds the waves approach rapidly or even very rapidly and the reduced time factor means that both the boat and the driver have less time to recognise and adapt to the changing wave patterns.

There is less time for the driver to make the necessary driving decisions, for the speed of the engines to vary under throttle control, and for the boat to change its attitude in relation to the waves. We will look at many of these aspects later, particularly engine and propulsion response, but the reduced time needed to respond to changing conditions can mean that they are not effective at higher speeds.

Left to its own devices and at a constant speed, a displacement boat will normally find its own solution to the changing wave patterns. In a planing boat there will be times when the speed at which the boat is running will be excessive for the conditions. Here you need to respond with the controls to help the boat negotiate the waves, always assuming that there is adequate time for the necessary changes to take place.

Then there is the question of navigation. Even at modest speeds of 1.6km (1 mile) every two minutes, the navigation situation will be changing quite rapidly and you need to focus to keep on top of the situation.

Finally there is the increased stress on the boat and its crew that comes from higher speeds. Again you can help here by intelligent use of the controls, but the condensed time frame can mean that you have little time to recover from one wave impact before the next.

When speeds move above the 40-knot mark, the time factor assumes increased importance. Driving at these speeds does mean that you have to appreciate fully just how quickly things can change. The reduced time available for every decision and every response does not allow time to relax. Indeed, if you find yourself relaxing in a boat travelling at over 40 knots it could be argued that you're not doing the driving job properly. In open waters there may not be anything close by to give the impression of the reduced time scale and it's only when you are operating in crowded waters that the difference becomes apparent as other craft and navigation features rush by. It can be difficult to imagine what it must be like when racing at 120 knots or more.

You don't have the luxury of time in a fast boat and it is important to recognise this at an early stage because the short time available will govern much of the way you operate the boat.

AT HIGH SPEEDS THINGS HAPPEN VERY QUICKLY AND YOU NEED TO FOCUS ON THE DRIVING AS WELL AS THE NAVIGATION.

# 2 SAFETY MARGINS

Driving a fast boat in calm conditions is pretty straightforward. Once you get the boat up onto the plane you can largely set the throttle and let the boat go – except, of course, you always need to be prepared for the unexpected, such as debris in the water or the wash of passing ships. Once waves come into the reckoning, the whole scenario changes. Not only do you need to trim the boat to match the conditions but you also need to take into account that waves are rarely regular and in any wave train you will get larger than average and smaller than average waves. The smaller than average waves are not going to be a problem but it is those larger ones that you need to focus on and build in a safety margin.

The problem with larger than average waves is that you are unlikely to recognise them until they are virtually on you. In some cases they can be transient and disappear before the boat encounters them – and in the same way they can appear at short notice right in front of the boat.

Because of the varying and largely unpredictable nature of the waves you can encounter, you don't want to operate the boat right on its limits, and you need to build safety margins into your driving of the boat so that you have something in reserve should that larger than average wave suddenly appear.

We tend to focus on larger than average waves, but for every larger wave there can also be deeper than average troughs. These deeper troughs are a worrying phenomenon because you won't see and recognise them until you virtually fall into them. A larger than average wave may be sighted two or three waves ahead but that deep trough will only be recognised when you come over the crest of the wave that precedes it.

Driving a fast boat right on its limits is exciting and this is what you do when racing, but in normal cruising operations you want to keep something in reserve. The main reserve that you have to play with is the speed of the boat, so easing back on the speed immediately builds a reserve of performance. The question is how much of a reserve do you need?

A lot will depend on the prevailing sea conditions and the response time of the boat but a reduction in speed of 5 knots from the maximum – or, say, 10% less than the flat-out speed for the conditions – would be appropriate to give you a margin of safety against the unexpected. Like most things associated with fast boats, there are no hard and fast rules, but you will know when you are driving on the limit and when you feel that you have a comfortable margin. Taking that hard edge off the speed will also make life on board more comfortable for the boat and its crew.

IN STORMY CONDITIONS YOUR SAFETY MARGINS BECOME QUITE SMALL.

# 3 REACTIONS AND RESPONSE TIMES

Unless the conditions are very good with a near flat calm, you will not be able to relax when driving a fast boat. Even in calm conditions you will need to be aware of the unexpected happening, such as the wash of a ship arriving in your path. In most cases when there are waves, the conditions will be constantly changing, and you will rarely find regular wave patterns where you can set the controls and let the boat take its course. On larger powerboats this can be possible, but on smaller craft up to, say, 12m (40ft) in length you will have to drive the boat with constant adjustments to the controls to optimise performance.

Two factors come into the reckoning here. First of all, it will take you time to assess the change taking place, perhaps the height and shape of a particular wave that the boat is encountering. This is called the reaction time. Then there is the time that it takes to work out your response to the situation in terms of what adjustments, if any, are necessary to the controls, and then to implement that action. This is called the response time; added to that there's also the time it will take for the engines to respond.

If you add the reaction and response times together, you have the time that it will take you to safely negotiate that particular wave. We are talking here about very short time intervals, normally fractions of a second, and when you are skilled at fast-boat driving the reaction and response times will be very small indeed. However, even an experienced driver will still be dependent on the response of the boat itself. A big heavy boat with diesel power is likely to be a slow responder, which is why it is common with such boats just to set the throttle at a comfortable speed and let the boat take its course. Any change in the throttle setting is unlikely to take place in time for it to be effective.

You will probably not even be aware of any time lapse in taking the necessary action and it is true that at 30 knots there is plenty of apparent time to take the action. When the speed of the boat increases to, say, 50 knots then the time available is halved and things start to get more critical. Again skill and experience have their part to play here, but the positioning of the controls and their ready availability for action are also important. To get the best performance from any type of powerboat you should assess what its response time is likely to be, particularly the time lag between engine commands and engine and propulsion response, because this can have a significant impact on the way you drive the boat. These factors will be discussed in later sections of the book.

# CONCENTRATION 4

The sea presents a constantly varying scenario with the conditions changing from minute to minute. Adapting the boat and its speed to cope with the changes requires a considerable amount of concentration if you wish to avoid getting caught out by the unexpected.

Concentration is a vital aspect of fast boat driving and you need to focus entirely on the advancing waves and the way in which the boat responding to them. Good concentration can reduce your reaction and response times considerably but you need the right environment and the right focus in order to maintain good concentration. Good visibility from the helm is a prime requirement – if you cannot easily see the advancing waves, you will be less able to respond to them. Spray on the windscreen, reflections and wide screen pillars can all reduce your vision and these irritations will make it harder to concentrate.

An array of navigation and monitoring screens in front of you can be distracting – this can be made worse if you have to do the navigation as well as drive the boat. Badly placed controls, such as the wheel and the throttle, and uncomfortable seating can have an effect on your concentration too. If you are steering the boat by compass, to steer effectively you will need to spend much time focusing on the compass and this can affect your level of concentration on the approaching waves. Using an autopilot for the steering can help considerably but not everyone is comfortable steering by autopilot in a fast boat, particularly a smaller one.

If you realise that it is becoming difficult to focus on both driving the boat and assessing the outside conditions, this is when you need to build in greater safety margins by reducing speed. If larger than average waves or those deeper troughs catch you unawares and cause violent movements of the boat, you won't travel any faster than if you had reduced speed in the first place. So be aware if there are things that are affecting your level of concentration and increase the safety margins in your driving to compensate.

A DIRTY WINDSCREEN AND WIDE PILLARS CAN AFFECT YOUR LEVELS OF CONCENTRATION.

# 5 BEFORE YOU LEAVE

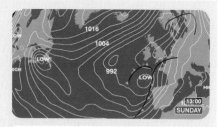

GETTING A GOOD-QUALITY WEATHER FORECAST IS AN ESSENTIAL PART OF YOUR PREPARATION.

As we have seen, when you are driving a fast powerboat in waves you need to focus on driving and handling the boat. However, you still need to be going in the right direction so navigating is important, and there are the engines to monitor and the systems to check. You will have a busy time, at least until you settle down on a steady course, so anything you can prepare before you leave harbour is time well spent.

Getting good weather information is important and you need the best-quality forecast you can get. From this you can assess what the sea conditions will be like (as shown in Anticipating the Waves, 50) but you also need to know what the tides will be doing. Wind against tide can make conditions a lot worse when the tides are strong, so look along your route to see where you might expect difficult conditions, such as around headlands and in narrow channels, and consider alternatives.

You can also do a lot of your navigation work before you leave. Whether you are using paper or electronic charts, setting out the courses and possible times along each leg of the route will save you work out at sea. Look at alternative destinations in case the conditions out there change or you encounter problems with the boat.

The third task before you go is to set up the radar, the autopilot and the radios to make sure that everything is working. You will want to set the radar on a useful range for working out at sea and this is likely to be the 5 or 10km (3 or 6 mile) range. You can often set the required course on the autopilot before you leave so that all you need to do when you clear the harbour is engage it.

You should certainly check the engines before you leave as well as the steering to make sure that it is fully operational. Carry out a check around the boat to ensure that any loose items are stowed and all the portholes are closed and secured. Finally, when you let go from the berth ensure that the mooring ropes and fenders are fully stowed so that they will not snake overboard into the propellers.

There always seems to be a rush to get going and in your haste it's easy not to carry out all the checks and preparation. However, it doesn't take much time, and these are tasks that are easy to do in harbour and often difficult to do at sea. Doing this preparation before you leave should save you having to stop out at sea to fix things and, more importantly, you should have all the information you need for navigation readily available so that you can focus on driving the boat.

THERE IS A LOT OF CHECKING TO DO BEFORE YOU HEAD OUT INTO THE OPEN SEA.

# 6 DEPTH OF VEE

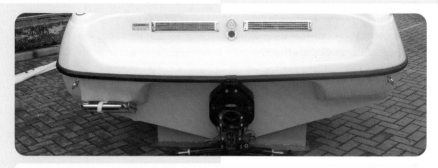

THE MODERATE VEE OF THIS SPORTS-BOAT HULL ALLOWS HIGHER SPEEDS BUT IT WILL REDUCE THE COMFORT LEVELS IN WAVES.

When you look at powerboats at a boat show, all the emphasis tends to be on what is above the waterline rather than what is below. It is the area below that determines how comfortable the boat will be at sea and how it will perform in waves. In calm water you could have a virtually flat surface under the water to make the boat plane, but it is performance in waves that counts and the underwater hull shape plays a significant part in this.

Probably 90% of modern powerboats are based on a vee hull. This is one where the bottom surfaces are shaped to form a vee when you see a cross section. This vee or deadrise angle determines to what degree the hull is cushioned against wave impact. The deeper the vee, the smoother the ride. A well-cushioned ride will insulate you from wave impact to a considerable degree.

However, it's not quite that simple. You could have a deadrise angle of, say, 20 degrees or more that would work well as a cushion – but it would also require more power to achieve the same speed. The most efficient planing surface is a flat plank where the water flowing past generates the maximum lift. You need this lift to get as much of the hull out of the water as possible to reduce the frictional resistance. Once there is a vee in the bottom of the hull, the lift generated is deflected sideways. That provides the cushion but is not so good for lift.

This is the dilemma that faces powerboat designers and these days we are seeing many of them taking the easy option of having a low deadrise so that they can improve the top speed with the same engine power. A deadrise of, say, 10 degrees will be pretty efficient as far as generating lift is concerned, but you will end up with a harsher ride in waves. Remember that you will rarely operate your boat at full speed, so efficient performance may not be as important as many builders would have us believe.

A good compromise for the deadrise would be around 15 degrees on a motor cruiser but on a smaller sports boat, where you will be more interested in driving the boat faster in waves, a deadrise of 20 degrees or more would be appropriate. Generally, the smaller the boat, the more deadrise you need because small boats are much more susceptible to wave influence.

THE DEEP VEE HULL OF THIS RACE BOAT IS HELPING TO CUSHION THE IMPACT WITH WAVES.

In some cases designers will introduce a deep vee and then compensate by introducing wide chines. These are flat surfaces that are placed where the bottom of the hull meets the topsides and they are there partly to help stabilise the hull, but also to generate more lift. On a motor cruiser these chines should be no more than about 10cm (4in) across, otherwise this flat surface will also generate heavy wave impacts.

Finally, when looking for a boat that is comfortable at sea, look at the bow shape. In order to get as much internal space as possible, designers will introduce a fat, full bow that has to force its way through waves, and the extra buoyancy here will tend to make the bow lift over the wave rather than drive through it. The result will be increased pitching in a head sea which will make life uncomfortable. On the other hand, a bow that is too fine could compromise the performance in following seas by burying deep into the waves.

Designers should aim for a balanced hull – one that will cope with the wide variety of conditions at sea. The problem is that internal space seems to be taking priority these days – which might just explain why some boat builders keep the underwater bits of their hulls covered up at boat shows!

# THE BENEFIT OF STEPS

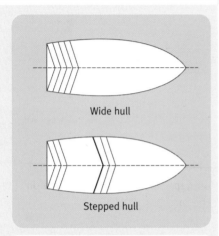

Wide hull

Stepped hull

THE TOP DIAGRAM SHOWS THE AMOUNT OF A HULL WITHOUT STEPS IN CONTACT WITH THE WATER AND THE LOWER ONE SHOWS HOW THE CONTACT IS SPLIT WITH A STEPPED HULL TO GIVE BETTER LONGITUDINAL STABILITY.

Fitting steps into the hull of a fast boat is nothing new and it dates back to the very early days of planing boats. However, steps were discontinued quite quickly because they were not easy to design into a wooden hull. They reappeared in the 1980s when they were first fitted to a deep vee hull. Even then steps were mainly used on racing and high-performance hulls but now, as the benefits of hull steps are more widely appreciated, they are finding their way into the hulls of production boats.

A few hulls have just one step but most modern production hulls use two steps. A hull without steps, such as a conventional deep vee, will ride on the planing surfaces extending forward from the transom at speed. This means that it is riding on planing surfaces that revolve around this single pivot point at the transom. When steps are fitted the planing surfaces are divided up into two or more areas so that there is much less focus on a single pivot point. This means that a stepped hull will be less prone to pitching and will tend to have a more level ride, which in turn improves the efficiency.

When a boat is planing, the lift generated by the hull is balanced by the weight of the boat, which will act around the centre of gravity. With just a single planing surface, the centre of gravity and the centre of lift have to be carefully balanced, but when steps are fitted there is more flexibility in the location of the centre of gravity and factors such as the position of varying weights, like those of the fuel and water tanks, are not so critical. However, it is important not to have too much weight on the steps – this can make the steering of the boat more sensitive, as the steering will pivot around the step rather than the transom.

Properly designed steps also allow air to be drawn in under the hull and this can help to lubricate the planing surfaces to make them more efficient. This air lubrication helps to reduce the friction between the hull and the water, which creates considerable friction resistance as speeds get higher. This advantage of steps explains why they have tended to be used only on very high-speed hulls in the past. Air lubrication could affect the performance of the propellers but the air doesn't create a problem with the surface-piercing propellers normally used on fast boats. However, having steps in the hull means that they will not work with water jet propulsion, which is

very intolerant to any air flowing into the jet intakes.

In summary, then, steps in the hull can promote a more level ride with less pitching and can also improve performance efficiency. With composite hulls there are none of the difficulties of incorporating steps in the hull that occur with wood and metal hulls but the focus on steps is still mainly for their use on high-performance hulls.

A STEPPED HULL IS SUPPORTED ON TWO OR MORE POINTS TO GIVE IMPROVED FORE AND AFT STABILITY.

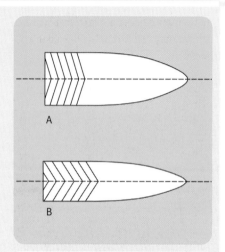

THE PLANING SURFACE OF A (A BEAMY BOAT) AND B (A NARROW–BEAMED BOAT). THE BEAMY BOAT HAS A MORE EFFICIENT PLANING SURFACE, BUT THE NARROW–BEAMED BOAT CUSHIONS WAVE IMPACT MORE EFFECTIVELY.

At any speed, a certain area of the hull needs to be in contact with the water to generate the necessary lift. The area in contact with the water will decrease as the speed rises. The area remaining in contact with the water to generate the lift will extend further forward on a hull with a narrow beam than it would on a hull with a wide beam. The more the contact area is concentrated aft, the less stable the hull will become and the more prone it will be to pitching and porpoising (see Porpoising, 37). This is because it only requires a small change in the longitudinal trim of the hull to generate a significant difference in the position of the centre of lift so that the boat becomes sensitive to trim and gives an uncomfortable ride.

On boats that have a speed up to around 40 knots, a wide beam can be acceptable because there will still be a considerable amount of the hull in contact with the water. As the speeds rise, this contact area decreases and it is only by narrowing the beam that a sufficient length of the hull forward from the transom remains in contact with the water.

The use of a narrower beam in the design of high-performance boats will also help to reduce slamming at speed, particularly in a head sea. The disadvantage of a narrow beam is that it

If you study the hulls of powerboats, you will notice that slower boats tend to have a wider beam and faster boats a narrow beam. This is partly explained by the fact that slower boats tend to require good internal space for accommodation, but performance also comes into play. To understand this, you need to think about the planing surfaces on which the hull is riding when it is at planing speeds. Depending on the speed, the boat rides on a section of the hull extending forward from the transom, and the amount of the hull that remains in contact with the water will depend on the speed of the boat and the width of the beam.

reduces the internal space available for accommodation, but this tends to assume less importance on high-performance boats and performance is the primary factor that the designer will focus on.

A WIDE HULL LIKE THIS OFFERS GOOD INTERNAL SPACE, BUT WILL GIVE A HARSHER RIDE.

A NARROWER HULL GIVES A BETTER RIDE AT HIGH SPEEDS.

# 9 SPRAY RAILS AND CHINES

THIS DEEP VEE HULL SHOULD GIVE A COMFORTABLE RIDE IN WAVES.

The spray rails and chines that are a feature of deep vee hulls are fitted to fine-tune the boat's performance. There are many variations in their design and an understanding of how they work will give a better appreciation of the merits of various hull designs.

The straightforward deep vee, where the smooth bottom panels meet the topsides, would work but it could lack stability. To improve the design, the chine was introduced at the point where the bottom meets the topsides; the angled bottom panels flatten out into a narrow horizontal strip at the meeting point. This strip serves two main purposes: to direct the water flow clear of the hull and to generate additional lift. The chines towards the bow will do most of the work in deflecting the water away from the hull, while the flat surfaces further aft generate the extra lift to help the boat

onto the plane and stabilise the hull. Because the chines are located low on bottom, they help to prevent the hull from heeling over. If it heels, the flat surface of the chines becomes an inverted vee and this generates even more lift on the down side of the hull so stability is assured. This stabilising effect, combined with the deflection of the water cleanly away from the hull to reduce the frictional resistance, makes a significant improvement to the performance of the hull.

Spray rails perform a similar function lower down on the angled panels of the hull. Here they deflect the water away from the hull at the earliest possible moment so that it has the minimum amount of contact with the hull surfaces. This will reduce frictional resistance. They also help to keep down the spray – hence their name. Because they run down the length of the hull,

**FAST BOAT DESIGN**

spray rails improve the directional stability of the hull. On very fast boats where the chine may come clear of the water, the spray rail acts as a secondary chine to help stabilise the hull at speed.

So the basic function of these two design features is to help stabilise the hull and make it more efficient, but they vary considerably from boat to boat. Wide chines and spray rails with a large horizontal area would obviously be the most efficient, but then you would get slamming on the flat surfaces and a harsh ride. Some chines are even angled down at their outer edges to make them more effective, but these deflect water away from the hull less efficiently, thereby increasing slamming and giving a rough ride. Every designer has his own thoughts about the best way to achieve good results, which is why you see so many variations of design; but there's no getting away from the fact that the larger the horizontal area, the harsher the ride will be.

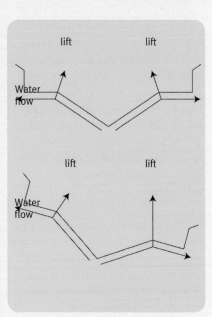

HOW SPRAY RAILS HELP TO STABILISE THE DEEP VEE HULL BY INCREASING THE LIFT ON THE LOWER SIDE OF THE HULL WHEN IT IS HEELED.

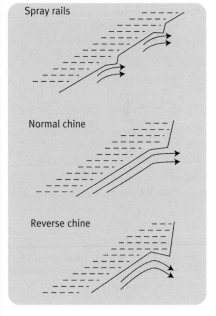

THE WAY SPRAY RAILS AND CHINES DIVERT THE WATER FLOW COMING AWAY FROM THE HULL.

# 10 CATAMARANS AND TRIMARANS

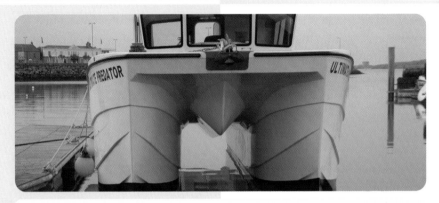

A CATAMARAN WITH A HIGH CROSS DECK THAT WILL REDUCE WAVE IMPACT.

There can be advantages in having more than one hull on a powerboat and there are increasing numbers of multihull powerboats on the market. Both catamarans and trimarans can offer higher efficiency and better stability, which is the main reason catamarans are among the fastest racing boats. However, multihulls also have disadvantages.

In The Effect of Beam, 8 we looked at the benefits of a narrow beam and both cats and tris exploit this by having long narrow hulls. Catamaran hulls usually have steps so that they offer a more level ride and this contributes considerably towards propulsion efficiency. The main disadvantage of using a mutihull is the loss of internal volume so it becomes harder to incorporate useful accommodation. This

is probably why multihulls have never become a major part of the powerboat scene. With multihulls, the space within the side hulls is limited and additional space for accommodation has to be added on top of the hulls rather than inside them.

There are two versions of both cats and tris, the ones that use a displacement hull and those with a planing hull. The displacement hull versions tend to have rounded hull forms and these rely on the low resistance of the long thin hull shape to carve an efficient path through the water. This allows them to be effective at speeds up to around 30 knots, although the longer the hull the higher the speed potential. Displacement hulls can be very fuel-efficient and seaworthy and have formed the basis of some long-range cruising powerboats.

The planing multihull has angled underwater surfaces and planes on these surfaces in the same way as a monohull. This allows much higher speeds and the efficiency of the catamaran is increased by the air lift that is generated by the air passing through the tunnel between the hulls. This lift reduces the amount of the hull that is in contact with the water and so reduces the frictional resistance of the hull. At really high speeds there is a delicate balance between this air lift and the stability of the hull,which has to be controlled by sensitive use of the throttle. It is the effect of this air lift that explains why fast catamarans can have a higher speed when heading into the wind than when heading downwind.

When comparing catamarans and trimarans, a general rule is that the catamaran is used where high speeds are required while the trimaran tends to be a more seaworthy design. The seaworthiness of a catamaran in waves can be compromised when the waves start to impact on the cross deck between the hulls. If the speed is reduced at this point, the hulls will sink lower in the water and the impact increases so that a catamaran will tend to have a quite sudden cut-off point where the seaworthiness deteriorates quite markedly.

Trimarans, on the other hand, tend to have the cross deck linking the hulls located well aft, with the side hulls being little more than stabilisers. This means that the long thin centre hull presents a small aspect to oncoming waves and will tend to pierce the waves to give a level ride rather than contour over them as a monohull might.

So multihulls can have advantages where high speed or good seaworthiness is the priority, but for general all-round use the monohull remains the best solution for most requirements.

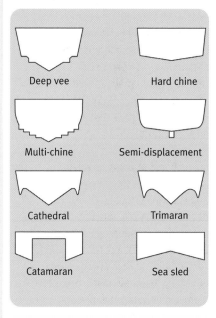

Deep vee     Hard chine

Multi-chine     Semi-displacement

Cathedral     Trimaran

Catamaran     Sea sled

THE WIDE VARIETY OF HULL SHAPES FOUND ON PLANING BOATS.

# 11 WHAT KEEPS YOUR BOAT STABLE?

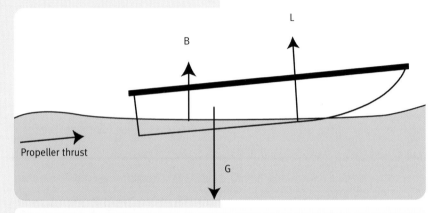

THE FORCES THAT ACT ON A PLANING BOAT. THE UPWARD FORCES OF LIFT AND BUOYANCY BALANCE OUT THE DOWNWARD FORCE OF GRAVITY. L = LIFT, G = CENTRE OF GRAVITY AND B = CENTRE OF BUOYANCY.

We take it for granted that a boat will stay reasonably upright at sea. If you move from side to side in the boat it will heel slightly and waves will cause the boat to heel, but it always comes back upright again. What is this hidden force that keeps the boat stable in a changing environment?

To understand this it is necessary to look at some of the basics of naval architecture. A boat at rest in the water has a weight that acts downwards through the centre of gravity. This weight is supported by the buoyancy of the water, which acts upwards through the centre of buoyancy. This centre of buoyancy is the geometric centre of the underwater section of the hull.

At rest, these two forces balance each other out and the boat is stable. The centre of gravity remains in the same place whatever angle the boat might adopt. It will only change its position if a weight is added or taken off the boat or moved within it. The centre of gravity may change slightly as you use up fuel or change some other weight in the boat, but for practical purposes it is static.

However, the centre of buoyancy can change considerably, particularly when the boat heels. Now the centre of buoyancy will move towards the downward side of the hull in order to maintain its location at the geometric centre of the underwater hull. With the force of buoyancy acting upwards and gravity acting downwards, and with the boat heeling, the two

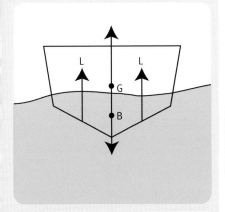

TRANSVERSE FORCES ACTING ON A PLANING BOAT. WHEN THE BOAT IS ON AN EVEN KEEL THE LIFT FACTORS BALANCE EACH OTHER TO KEEP THE BOAT UPRIGHT.

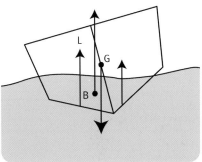

WHEN A PLANING BOAT HEELS, THE LIFT FACTOR ON THE LOWER SIDE IS INCREASED, THUS PRODUCING AN ADDITIONAL RIGHTING FORCE IN ADDITION TO THAT GENERATED BY THE MOVEMENT OF THE CENTRE OF BUOYANCY.

forces are now out of line. The upward force of buoyancy has moved to the lower side of the hull, while the centre of gravity has remained in the same place. This prompts a righting movement that will bring the hull upright until the two forces are once more in line. You get the same effect if a wave attacks the hull on one side. The centre of buoyancy moves to that side and causes the hull to heel, but in heeling equilibrium is again restored and the hull comes upright once the wave has passed.

This stabilising effect is a constant balancing act that takes place automatically. The situation is more complex on a planing boat because here the hull is also supported by the lift from the planing surfaces. When upright, this lift is equally balanced on both sides, but when the boat heels there is a higher proportion of the lift on the lower side and once more the hull will come upright – assisted, of course, by the shift in the centre of buoyancy.

You get the same effects to a smaller extent in the fore and aft direction, but here the centre of lift comes more into the equation. This centre of lift is usually located a short distance behind the point where the waterline meets the hull and the centres of lift and buoyancy will move forward and aft to keep the boat in balance. While this balancing action takes place automatically, the driver can exert some control by using the secondary controls, as we shall see later in the book.

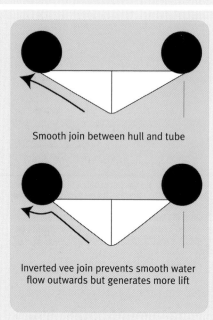

Smooth join between hull and tube

Inverted vee join prevents smooth water flow outwards but generates more lift

ALTERNATIVE RIB HULL FORMS.

RIBs have taken the powerboat market by storm, in spite of their normally higher cost and heavier weight. Probably 50% of the smaller new boats entering the market are RIBs and their popularity is easy to see when the benefits of a correctly designed and operated RIB are appreciated.

With the increased beam when the boat is at rest, stability is greatly improved. As the boat lifts onto the plane, the inflatable tubes should come clear of the water and the hull behaves just like a regular deep vee with a relatively long and narrow hull. To get this advantage, the tubes should just touch the water when the boat is at rest. If the tubes are too low, they will not clear the water as the boat lifts. If set too high, there will be no benefit when the boat is at rest as the hull would have to heel over a considerable way before the tubes touch the water.

If the boat heels or encounters a wave on one side when travelling at speed, the tube on the low side generates plenty of reserve buoyancy and quickly brings the boat back upright. It is important that the tube is at the right pressure – normally around 2 psi. If the pressure is too high, the tube will 'bounce' on the water and generate an uncomfortable ride. In extreme situations,  you could end up with the boat bouncing from side to side. If the tube pressure is too low, however, there will be too much 'give' for it to be fully effective and it will deform rather than generate the required lift.

Another advantage is that the tube can act as a built-in fender for the boat. This can be beneficial when going alongside another boat at sea, which is one of the reasons that RIBs are widely used as rescue boats. Again, if the tube pressure is too high the boat will 'bounce' when it comes alongside, and it will be very difficult to hold in position.

This shock-absorbing characteristic of the inflatable tube can also assist the seaworthiness of the RIB. At the correct pressure, the tube will absorb some of the shock of impact with waves, particularly around the bow, with the tube varying its shape to a degree in order to match the shape of the wave. This form of variable geometry gives the properly designed RIB some of its unique characteristics.

Overall, then, a RIB is both safer and more seaworthy than a regular powerboat. It is virtually unsinkable because of its many individual air compartments, while its stability at low speed makes it good as a diving boat.

THIS RIB IS BEING STABILISED IN ITS TURN BY THE TUBE ON THE INSIDE, WHICH RESTRICTS HEELING.

# 13 MAKE SURE YOU CAN SEE

When driving a powerboat at speed it is essential that you have good all-round visibility. However, there are many powerboats where visibility is not ideal and with these you need extra caution and perhaps slower speeds.

The best view will always be from an open helm, such as you often find in a RIB or small powerboat, or at the top helm of a flybridge cruiser. Once you put a windscreen in front of the driver, visibility will start to deteriorate, and with a fully enclosed helm the visibility can be quite poor.

It is often the structure supporting the windscreen that reduces visibility from the helm. On many open fast boats the designers like to offer the option of looking over or through the windscreen. It sounds desirable, but you can end up with a situation where the top bar of a windscreen may be set just at eye level so that you are forced to stretch to look over it or crouch to look through it. Faced with this situation, you won't be focusing fully on the sea conditions ahead. If you have to look through the screen then salt, spray or rain on the glass can seriously reduce visibility. Further problems can come from reflections on the glass of an angled windscreen when it picks up the sun shining on the fascia below. These

reflections can be particularly bad when the screen is tinted.

These problems also occur with a fully enclosed helm, where the side supports of the screen can obstruct visibility. These supports are often wide enough to block out an arc of 15 or 20 degrees of visibility range and can make it difficult to spot other vessels or read the waves in a beam sea.

All these visibility problems become more acute at night. Reflections from lights on the dashboard or from the saloon behind can reduce the clear view through the screen.

THE WIDE WINDSCREEN PILLARS ON THIS BOAT CREATE A CONSIDERABLE BLIND SPOT FOR THE DRIVER.

**UNDERSTANDING YOUR BOAT**

The height of the outboards on the transom is usually predetermined by the builder. The normal setting for the cavitation plate would be level with, or slightly above, the bottom of the hull at the transom.

Some high-performance craft have an adjustable mounting plate. This allows the height of the outboard to be adjusted when you are under way, so that the propeller can operate in surface-piercing mode. Even when you have a permanent height setting for the outboard, it is possible to raise it a few centimetres to get better performance; but this will be at the expense of low-speed performance and the boat may have difficulty getting onto the plane.

Adjusting the toe-in, the relative angle between the two outboards of a twin installation, can be done by an owner. Rather than have the two outboards lying parallel, if they are angled in at the rear end by a few degrees, the propulsion thrust will be more efficient. The adjustment is done on the tie rod that links the two engines for the steering and it is best done at sea. When running at speed, the wake from each engine should meet at a point between 1½ and 2 boat lengths behind.

The torque tab, located at the rear of the cavitation plate, above and behind the propeller, can be adjusted to introduce a steering effect on the outboard to compensate for the sideways prop thrust. Adjustment is made by the clamping bolt at the top, and on a single outboard installation it will usually need to be set at an angle of between 5 and 10 degrees. Assuming that you have the normal clockwise turning propeller when viewed from behind, the torque tab should be angled towards the starboard side, as the boat will naturally turn to port. You will know when you have the angle right because any pull on the steering wheel will disappear.

If you use the boat for water-skiing you might find a higher angle for the tab setting better, because there will be more propeller torque with the tow behind. With a stern drive installation, the height will be fixed but the toe-in and the torque tab adjustments will still apply on twin and single installations.

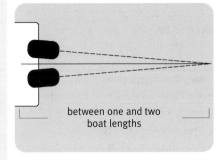

between one and two
boat lengths

HAVING A SLIGHT 'TOE IN' ON THE OUTBOARDS
IMPROVES EFFICIENCY.

# 15 FLAPS AND INTERCEPTORS

FLAPS CAN BE USED TO CONTROL BOTH THE TRANSVERSE AND THE FORE AND AFT TRIM.

Flaps (sometimes also called trim tabs) are the angled plates that are hinged at the bottom of the transom on each side. The flaps are normally hydraulically operated by switches or a joystick lever on the dashboard and they are used to adjust the trim of the boat. By angling the flaps downwards, they change the flow of the water under the transom and generate a lifting effect.

If you put both flaps down, the transom will lift evenly and effectively when the bow is lowered. You might want to do this on a heavily laden boat when it's coming onto the plane to generate extra lift to compensate for the extra weight. On many earlier surface-drive systems you had to use the flaps to get the boat onto the plane by generating extra lift.

However, the main use of lowering both flaps together in this way is when operating in head seas. Here the flaps are lowered in order to help to keep the bow down and stop it 'flying' as it lifts to the waves. You can get a more comfortable ride by using the flaps, but keeping the bow down can generate more spray from the hull – so, like most techniques with fast boats, you need to find the right balance.

Using the flaps in unison adjusts the longitudinal trim, while the flaps are used individually to adjust the transverse trim of the hull. Put one flap down and the hull is lifted on the side where the flap is down. You would normally use this adjustment to counteract heeling from propeller torque (see Torque Reaction, 18) or when the boat is heeling into the wind (see Heeling into the Wind, 28), both situations where you can get a more comfortable ride if the boat is riding level.

When you do put one flap down in this way you will find that it will also affect the steering, because the lowered flap creates more drag on the side of the boat where it is lowered. You will need to counteract this drag by adding in a few degrees extra on the steering wheel. This procedure can be used as a form of emergency steering – you won't maintain a very steady course because flaps tend to be slow-acting. Because of the slow response time, it will be hard to find the right level of adjustment, but it could get you home.

Interceptors are vertical plates attached to the extremities of the transom that can be lowered a small amount below the transom. They do much the same job as flaps and are adjusted in the same way, but they are more efficient because they offer less resistance when they are generating the lift and they are usually faster-acting. This quicker response has allowed interceptors to form part of a

ride-control system where the trim of the boat is adjusted automatically in response to commands from a computer.

Rocker switches are the usual form of control for flaps and interceptors – push the front end of the switch and the bow goes down; push the rear end and the bow lifts. Usually the port switch controls the port flap, which is the logical way to operate it, but on some installations the operation is reversed – you push the switch on the side that you want the bow to go down, which activates the flap on the opposite side.

INTERCEPTORS ARE AN ALTERNATIVE TO FLAPS AND ARE FASTER ACTING.

# 16 PROPELLERS

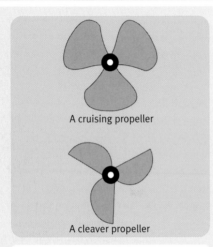

A cruising propeller

A cleaver propeller

THE DIFFERENT TYPES OF PROPELLER FOUND ON FAST BOATS.

The propellers are probably the most critical part of the whole boat in terms of efficiency. It is the propeller that transforms the power of the engine into propulsive thrust and you will lose a lot of the efficiency if the boat has the wrong propeller. Equally important, when the correct propeller is fitted, is to keep it in good condition – a propeller with a ragged edge through grounding or hitting debris or one that is covered with barnacles will lose effectiveness quite dramatically. You can clean a propeller and restore the edges with a file or by grinding.

Even with experts there is a degree of trial and error involved in choosing the right prop. In many cases, the diameter of the propeller is controlled by the size of the propeller aperture, so the only remaining factor within your control is the pitch of the blades.

The pitch is the distance the propeller will move forward in one revolution. To check whether the pitch is approximately correct, run the engine at its maximum rpm in calm water. If the rpm corresponds with the maximum rpm given in the engine handbook, then the propeller pitch is about right. If the rpm runs high then a larger-pitch propeller might be required, and if too low then the propeller pitch is probably too large.

Many factors will affect rpm readings – the cleanliness of the bottom of the boat, the loading of the boat and, in the case of outboards and stern drives, the trim angle of the drives. Now you can start to see why choosing the right propeller is a complex business. If you run the boat in rough seas a lot of the time, or if you regularly tow a water-skier, then you might want to fit a smaller-pitch propeller in order to get better acceleration.

The shape and type of propeller blades can also affect performance. A surface-piercing propeller is likely to be of the cleaver type with a sharp leading edge and a blunt trailing edge, because cavitation is not a problem with these

**UNDERSTANDING YOUR BOAT**

propellers. With fully submerged propellers, a more rounded shape is used that will give a smoother passage through the water. With outboards and stern drives, the engine exhaust is sometimes taken through the propeller hub, so here the hub has a much larger diameter. Controllable pitch propellers are being developed for use on surface drives, which allow the pitch of the propeller to be varied when under way. These have huge advantages, but ensuring the reliability of the highly stressed blades has delayed development.

A CORRODED PROPELLER WILL REDUCE ITS EFFICIENCY CONSIDERABLY.

SURFACE DRIVE PROPELLERS ON A FIXED DRIVE INSTALLATION.

# 17 PROPULSION RESPONSE

THIS DUOPROP STERN DRIVE SHOULD GIVE EXCELLENT ACCELERATION AND RESPONSE.

Just as the type of engine can affect the response time, so can the propulsion method. Again, it's mainly a question of the weight of components and the boat, but the size and type of propeller also come into the equation.

A small propeller will tend to allow faster acceleration than a larger one but there will always be a higher risk of cavitation with the smaller, faster-turning propeller. A propeller with a smaller pitch will allow faster acceleration than a propeller with a larger pitch. In looking at the question of pitch, it's easy to imagine that the smaller-pitch propeller will get a better 'bite' on the water while one with a larger pitch could start to cavitate initially under acceleration until the boat starts to increase speed to match.

Reducing the pitch on a propeller is a good way to get better acceleration, but you have to balance the improved acceleration against the possibility that the engine will be over-revving at full throttle or that the engine cut-out may operate. If you use the boat for water-skiing, a smaller pitch will help both to pull the skier out of the 'hole' and to balance the extra weight of the tow.

**UNDERSTANDING YOUR BOAT**

The time taken to feel the response of opening the throttle, usually an initial response of the bow lifting or falling, will also depend on the speed at which the boat is running. When operating at around two-thirds speed or more, with the boat fully on the plane, the response is likely to be quick because the propeller is already operating effectively. If the speed has slowed to the point where the boat is not fully on the plane, the response will be slower as the propeller thrust has to overcome the added resistance of getting the boat onto the plane before it can accelerate away.

It can be tempting when operating in a head sea to pull the throttle right back when encountering a larger wave, but this action is likely to reduce your freedom to accelerate quickly afterwards and you can find the boat wallowing as the engine tries to pick up speed. Short, sharp movements of the throttle should be enough to raise or lower the bow without too much loss of speed and this is the way to drive a fast boat if you are having to use the throttle in waves.

Surface propellers can be slower to accelerate than those fully submerged, partly because they usually have a high pitch but also because air is drawn into the propeller, which can slow down the time to when it 'bites' again. It can be particularly important with surface propellers not to reduce speed too much, particularly to the point where it might revert to operating in fully immersed mode.

SURFACE DRIVES LIKE THIS WILL GIVE A GOOD RESPONSE PROVIDED THAT THE BOAT REMAINS ON THE PLANE.

# 18 TORQUE REACTION

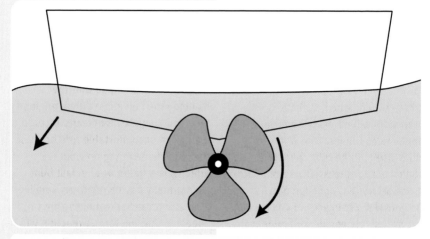

WITH THE PROPELLER TURNING CLOCKWISE, THE TORQUE REACTION WILL TEND TO MAKE THE BOAT HEEL TO PORT.

A propeller turning round and carving its way through the water needs something to react against if it is to be effective. With boats, it's the hull that provides the reaction against the propeller thrust when there's a single propeller. Here, turning the propeller in one direction tries to turn the hull of the boat in the other direction until the resistance of the hull to heeling counteracts the propeller torque and a balance is found. In practice, this means that in calm water the hull will heel over to one side and the increased buoyancy created on that side will provide the reaction against the propeller torque.

Heeling can be corrected by lowering the flap on the side towards which the hull

is heeling. This enables the boat to run upright again. However, this will then affect the steering because of the increased drag, so that a correction to the steering will be required to keep the boat on track. With a propeller turning in the normal clockwise direction looking from the stern, the hull will heel over to port, and with the port flap down the steering correction will need to be to starboard.

The torque reaction created by the propeller turning should not be confused with the sideways thrust that occurs because the lower blades of the propeller are in more 'solid' water than the top blades, so that the propeller wants to 'walk' sideways at the transom.

This effect is balanced by the thrust tab fitted to outboards and stern drives (as described in Setting up Outboards, 14) or, on slower boats, simply by a small adjustment on the steering.

With a twin-engine installation, the propellers will normally be turning in opposite directions. One will turn clockwise and the other anticlockwise, so that the torque reaction from each propeller will be cancelled out. Obviously if a twin screw boat is being run on a single engine for any reason you will experience both the torque reaction and the steering reaction, the latter caused by the offset propeller, and you will have to correct as described above.

The more power that is put into the propeller from the engine, the greater the torque reaction, so that the heeling effect on a fast single-engined boat can be quite significant. It could lead to an uncomfortable ride because the hull will be riding on what is effectively a flatter vee. A fast boat will normally have a relatively small-diameter propeller turning at high speed so that the torque reaction will be reduced, but where a large-diameter propeller is fitted, expect an increase in the torque reaction.

A TWIN PROPELLER INSTALLATION THAT PRODUCES ZERO STEERING TORQUE.

# 19 ENGINE RESPONSE

THE TYPE OF SMALL, FAST POWERBOAT WHERE A QUICK ENGINE RESPONSE IS IMPORTANT TO ENSURE GOOD HANDLING IN WAVES.

Engine response is a vital factor in fast powerboat driving. As we saw in Reaction and Response Times, 3, a quick engine response is vital in being able to control the boat in waves and making rapid progress. When considering engine response times, the actual time that it takes for you to make the throttle movement counts, but there is also the time that it takes for the engine and propulsion system to respond to your commands.

The type of response you get from the engine will depend a great deal on the type of engines you have. Petrol engines tend to have a quick response while diesels are slower, but response times are related more to the configuration of the engine than the type. A small lightweight engine will

always have a quicker response than a bigger, heavier engine because it takes more time for the heavier components in the bigger engine to react.

The fastest response will come from outboard engines, where the engine components tend to be very small. With these high-revving engines the response will be almost immediate, but you do need to know at what point in the rpm range of the engine the power comes in. You can find that on many high-performance engines the full power only comes in with the last 1,000 rpm of the rpm range and this can make driving the boat difficult. Not only will the throttle movement be limited to this last few rpm, but it will also be difficult to get sensitive control because the engine will tend to 'on' or 'off' power rather than a steady increase.

It is petrol engines that tend to have this more limited power range for throttle response. Generally, the more powerful the engines, the slower will be the response, although the slower response of a diesel engine is balanced by good low-speed torque, meaning that you should have a reasonable response throughout the rpm range. Any diesel engine over about 500hp will have a relatively slow response, so you won't get any benefits by trying to control the performance in waves by using the throttle.

Modern diesels with electronic control have an even slower response. This is because the electronic control tends to slow down the response to throttle movements electronically under the guise of helping to reduce the stresses on the engine and so preserve its life. A slower throttle response can also reduce fuel consumption.

The propulsion system can also affect the response time because that is what transmits the engine power to the water. With a small, fast-turning propeller, the response will be faster than with a larger, slower-turning propeller. There are many factors that affect response time and even the weight of the boat can come into the equation. Don't expect any exciting responses in a boat over 12m (40ft) unless it is specifically designed for high performance.

WITH ITS TWO POWERFUL OUTBOARDS, THIS BOAT SHOULD HAVE A QUICK ENGINE RESPONSE.

# 20 SEPARATE THROTTLE AND GEAR LEVERS

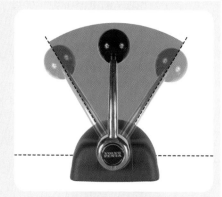

THIS PICTURE SHOWS THE ANGLE OF THE LEVER MOVEMENT BEFORE THE GEARS ARE ENGAGED.

The standard type of engine control has the throttle and gear controls combined into a single lever. This makes control of the boat easy for beginners and there is a certain logic in the system – just move the lever forward to engage gear and then continue to move it forward to increase speed. However, combining the two does not provide the best solution in terms of control and you will find that boats that have to operate in more extreme conditions will separate the control for the gears from the control of the throttle. Race boats always have the controls separated and this is also a feature of many sport fishing boats.

There are two main reasons for separating the two controls. When you are manoeuvring into a berth or operating at slow speed in confined waters, you will be using the engines only at idling speed almost all the time. If you want to nudge the boat ahead, you just engage the gear to give enough speed forward, so in this manoeuvring situation you are only using the gears and not the throttles. With separate levers there's no confusion and no risk of running past the gear-selection position on the lever and getting more speed than required. It can make manoeuvring in harbour a safer and more precise operation by using the gears only in this way.

Out at sea, the ahead gear is engaged and you will only be using the throttle to control the boat. Here, the big advantage of having separate levers is that there is a wider range of lever movement to cover the opening and closing of the throttle and this will give you more delicate control. When the gear and throttle controls are combined into a single lever, the range of throttle operation may be limited to just 30 degrees of arc – not much movement to cover speeds from idling to full ahead. The range of movement of the throttle has to be curtailed not only because of the initial movement to engage both ahead and astern gears, but also to allow for the downward movement that opens the throttle in astern gear.

Trying to accommodate this extensive range of movement into a control mounted on the dashboard can mean that the operation of the ahead range of throttle has to be restricted because it is well forward of the pivot point of the lever. You can find yourself reaching well forward to operate this critical section of the ahead range, so that delicate control is not possible. With a separate throttle lever, not only can the arc of throttle movement be extended but the position of the lever can also be optimised for best control and response in the critical areas.

When driving a fast boat, the section of the throttle operation that governs the top half of the range is the most critical, so this should be positioned where it is easiest to use. This would normally be with the half-throttle opening position being upright or slightly behind the upright position. Another advantage of using separate control levers is that the reduced movement required for the throttle lever allows a support pad to be placed behind the lever so that you can rest your arm on this to give more precise control. This will prevent you from making inadvertent movements of the throttle if the motion of the boat causes involuntary arm movements.

NORMALLY ONLY THE GEARS ARE USED FOR HARBOUR MANOEUVRING.

# 21 THE THROTTLE IS THE KEY

The throttle is the most important control in a powerboat. It controls the speed of the boat and helps control the trim, at least in the short term. When you are driving the boat in waves, apart from the steering wheel, the throttle is the main and probably only control you will use.

In normal driving conditions you will set the throttle at a comfortable speed where the boat will operate without excessive pitching and violent movements in the waves. This will give you an extra margin of speed to cope with any larger waves that come along and should give you a relatively smooth ride. The change in trim when you open and close the throttle can be felt if you try this in calm water. Open the throttle and the bow will lift because the extra power increases the lift from the planing surfaces. Close the throttle and the bow will drop as the lift decreases. The response to opening and closing the throttle is rapid and in the short term there will be virtually no effect on the speed of the boat. These quick trim changes are the key to fast boat driving and give you a more comfortable ride in adverse conditions.

With high-performance boats you can use changes in trim to help counteract the lift generated by the waves. A skilled driver will anticipate how the hull is going to be affected by the oncoming waves and counteract them by quick bursts on the throttle to maintain a level trim. That is the key to fast progress.

THE THROTTLE IS THE KEY TO DRIVING A FAST BOAT, SO GOOD LOCATION AND EASY OPERATION HELP CONSIDERABLY.

**THE PRIMARY CONTROLS**

How you use the throttle will depend a great deal on the type of boat you are driving. Don't expect an exciting response from a big heavy boat, because the weight of the boat will delay any reaction to an increase in power. You will eventually get control over the trim, but it may not be fast enough to react to passing waves. You may have little option but to find a comfortable setting for the throttle and let the boat run its course.

There will be much the same situation with most flybridge cruisers, and anything over 12m (40ft) or so in length will certainly have a reduced response unless it is a dedicated performance boat. The use of the throttle really comes into its own on smaller sports boats and RIBs, where you get that exciting immediate response.

Constant use of the throttle to help match the attitude of the boat to the oncoming waves requires delicate adjustment and the increased range of throttle movement found with separate control levers (as shown in Separate Throttle and Gear Levers, 20), can be a great help here. It's so easy to move the single throttle lever further than intended, and you can find yourself bringing the lever almost back to the idle position if you are not careful. This in turn means that the boat can come off the plane and you will have to wait as it struggles to get back up again. Even if the boat does not drop off the plane, you might find that the speed has dropped too far back to get the quick response that you need when you open the throttle again. When operating at speed in waves, you would normally want to operate the throttle lever in the range between full and half speed.

Ideally the throttle lever should be stiff enough to not move it inadvertently, but free enough to allow the quick response that you need. Cable control systems provide the right degree of stiffness, while the modern electronic throttles tend to have little or no resistance to movement and have very short levers, which restrict the ability for delicate control. The engine manufacturers may also build an electronic delay into the movement, so they are not the ideal system for fast boat use. However, you only tend to find them on larger powerboats where the throttle control is not so critical.

# 23 TYPES OF STEERING

Steering is one of the primary controls of a powerboat and obviously its main use is to point the boat in the right direction. However, the type of steering that is fitted to the boat will have an effect on the way you control it, with two main types normally being fitted.

Hydraulic steering is now used more and more on powerboats and is certainly the steering system of choice for most craft. By using hydraulics, it is a simple matter to add power assistance to the steering – and this can have good and bad effects. On the plus

A QUICK STEERING RESPONSE HELPS FOR HARBOUR MANOEUVRING, BUT YOU WILL WANT A SLOWER RESPONSE AT SEA.

THE PRIMARY CONTROLS

side, it makes the steering much lighter and easier to use because the power assistance is doing the work. On most boats with larger outboards and stern drives, power steering is a standard part of the equipment so there is no choice in the matter. These integrated systems work well, are thoroughly tested and reliable, and they let you spin the wheel with one finger.

The downside with power steering is that it takes all the feel out of the steering. There is no feedback, so you lose that intimate connection with the boat that can make you more sensitive to what is going on. Probably the main downside to power steering of this type is that the wheel will have only a limited movement from lock to lock, sometimes as little as one full turn, so it takes only a small movement of the wheel to have a significant effect. That is fine when you are manoeuvring in harbour, but out at sea it can lead to excessive steering corrections and that in turn can affect the trim of the boat. This is explained in more detail in The Effect of Steering on Trim, 24, but certainly very sensitive steering of this type can have an adverse effect on the behaviour of the boat.

Ideally the steering should have at least two turns from lock to lock to give the right level of sensitivity. When the propeller thrust is used for steering, as is the case with stern drives, outboards, water jets and many types of surface drive, there is a greater steering effect from only a small movement of the wheel and more turns from lock to lock could be a benefit here.

Wire and pulley steering is now virtually extinct but the push-pull cable type of steering is still used on some outboards and stern drives. This can give more sensitivity to the steering, but even with these systems, power steering is often introduced. When the steering system doesn't incorporate power steering, there may be a valve in the system that prevents feedback in order to stop the propeller torque from creating a heavy load or pull on the steering. Adjusting the torque fin on the outboard leg can help to balance out the torque effect and even when the 'zero torque' type of steering is used the torque fin should be set on any boat with a single engine (see photo in Torque Reaction, 18).

Most drivers will see a light steering system as a benefit – hence the widespread use of power steering. However, it does remove sensitive control of the boat, which can have adverse effects in rough seas and can even give a rougher ride as the boat heels from side to side under the influence of the steering.

# 24 THE EFFECT OF STEERING ON TRIM

When you power a boat into a turn, you will see that the boat heels into the turn under the effect of steering. The deeper the vee of the deadrise of the hull, the higher will be the angle of heel into the turn. This makes you feel very secure and comfortable when driving the boat and turning because it helps to balance the outward forces generated by the turn.

However, the negative effect of this is felt when operating in waves because when the boat heels into the turn, the inside section of the vee hull becomes nearly parallel with the sea surface. If you then hit waves, you can get some hard slamming on the hull – so ease the boat into a turn rather than execute very sharp turns.

There is also a negative effect when you are driving the boat in a straight line. Even the quite small movements of the wheel that are required to keep the boat on course can also affect the transverse trim and cause the boat to heel slightly under the influence of the helm. Again, the deeper the vee, the more sensitive the boat will be to these small movements of the wheel. A boat with a deep vee hull needs to remain upright to get the maximum benefit from the cushioning effect of the vee, and if the boat is heeling under the movements of the steering then you can expect a

rougher ride because the hull lands on a more horizontal surface when heeling.

On a boat where only a minimum of wheel movement is required to get a steering effect, this heeling is likely to be more pronounced because you are more likely to over-correct the steering. In this situation, very sensitive use of the wheel is needed and the solution will be largely in the hands of the person steering the boat. It's a question not just of using the minimum of wheel movement to get the required steering corrections but also of keeping the steering corrections to a minimum.

When operating in waves, the heading of the boat will be affected by the contact of the hull with waves and it's a natural instinct to try and correct these variations with the wheel. However, you will often find that the hull corrects itself, so rather than try to correct every small alteration of course, only focus on the corrections needed for longer-term rather than short-term variations, and this way you will get a smoother ride. Assuming that the boat has power steering, you can help this situation by only gripping the wheel lightly. If you grip it tightly, you will find that you make inadvertent corrections by using the wheel as a handhold to steady yourself against the movement of the boat. Hold the wheel gently and only make corrections when you see a distinct variation in course that needs correcting. Even then, make the necessary corrections a little at a time and with this technique you should see a considerable improvement in the ride.

Over-enthusiastic steering correction will cause the boat to heel from side to side in a very uncomfortable fashion and you should learn just to caress the wheel rather than use harsh movements.

THIS POWERBOAT IS HEELING INTO THE WIND AND THE TRIM CAN BE ADJUSTED WITH THE FLAPS.

# 25 POWER TRIM

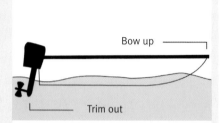

Bow up ——————

Trim out

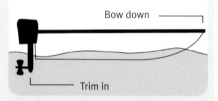

Bow down ——————

Trim in

THE EFFECTS OF TRIMMING IN AND TRIMMING OUT AN
OUTBOARD. THE SAME APPLIES TO STERN DRIVES.

Power trim is where the drive leg of an
outboard or a stern drive can be moved
in or out from the transom under
hydraulic power. This alters the angle at
which the propeller thrust is directed in
a vertical direction and provides another
means of trimming the boat.

Power trim works the opposite way to
flaps. Flaps can be used to move the
bow down but cannot lift it, while power
trim can be used to lift the bow. The
primary purpose of power trim is to
improve the performance rather than the
ride – but the two can go hand in hand.

When the drive leg is trimmed out, the

propeller thrust is angled up towards the
surface of the water and this forces the
stern of the boat down. This will in turn
lift the bow, and the fore and aft trim so
that there is less of the hull in contact
with the water. The boat will be
supported more by the planing surfaces
towards the stern and this reduces the
friction resistance of the hull to allow
higher speeds.

You do need to be quite sensitive when
using power trim because, as the hull
lifts to bring the planing surfaces and
the point of lift further aft, it can become
more unstable and liable to porpoise
(see Porpoising, 37). If you apply too
much power trim, the boat will be
supported by a relatively small section
of the hull aft and the bow can start to
rise and fall as the hull tries to find a
balance point. Porpoising will be more
noticeable in calmer water and is an
indication that the drive has been
trimmed out too far. It can normally be
corrected by trimming the drive slightly,
to get the correct balance.

Power trim would normally be used once
the boat has lifted onto the plane,
although on a heavily laden boat it could
be used earlier to help the boat get onto
the plane. Remember that trimming out
the drive leg also tends to bring the
propeller closer to the surface of the
water, creating a risk of cavitation, so

**THE SECONDARY CONTROLS**

any early application of trim has to be done sensitively. On a boat that has contra-rotating propellers of the type found on some stern-drive systems, the power trim adjustment is not so sensitive because these propellers are less prone to cavitation.

Practice finding the correct balance for the power trim in calm water, when you can see the effects of the adjustment more clearly. Once you have found the right setting for the regular loading conditions of the boat, with a bit of adjustment, this will also be suitable when driving through waves. Normally you will want to trim the drive leg in a little when making sharper turns and when encountering areas of rougher water; the drive should also be trimmed right in when slowing down and coming off the plane.

WHEN THE POWER TRIM IS SET UP CORRECTLY THE BOAT SHOULD RUN MORE EFFICIENTLY.

# 26 POWER TRIM FOR SURFACE DRIVES

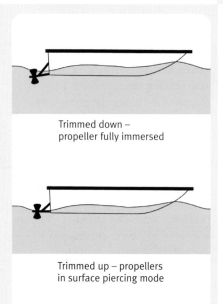

Trimmed down –
propeller fully immersed

Trimmed up – propellers
in surface piercing mode

A TRIMMABLE SURFACE DRIVE IN SUBMERGED AND
SURFACE PIERCING MODES.

There are several types of surface drive, such as the Arneson, where it is possible to trim the drive up and down under hydraulic control. Here you are moving the propeller up or down in relation to the transom rather than in or out as is the case with stern drives or outboards, but the effect is similar. Moving the propeller up alters the shaft angle and so the propeller thrust is directed more towards the surface of the sea when the drive is lifted. This produces the downward thrust on the transom that will lift the bow in much the same manner as with a stern drive.

The main reason for adjusting the angle of the drive shaft on a trimmable surface drive is to bring the propeller closer to the surface so that it starts to operate in surface-piercing mode. The propeller will move towards the surface anyway as the boat starts to lift onto the plane because the hull of the boat is lifting in the water, but with the trim adjustment you can fine-tune the height of the propeller for maximum efficiency and you can also lift the propeller to get it into surface-piercing mode at an early stage of the operation.

However, with a trimmable surface drive you have more freedom of adjustment than can be found with a stern drive because you can also lower the shaft line below the median point. This means that in theory it's possible to both raise and lower the bow of the boat by adjusting the angle of the drive shaft. This should give you more control over the trim of the boat, but in practice it would only be in more extreme seas that you might lower the bow in this way because by lowering the drive shaft you will take the propeller back into a fully submerged mode and that will slow the boat considerably.

One advantage of having a trimmable surface drive is that the trim action can be used to help get the boat onto the plane quickly. If the drive shaft is lifted

**THE SECONDARY CONTROLS**

slightly when the throttles are opened from rest, this reduces the loading on the engine because the propeller will start to cavitate as it switches into surface-piercing mode. This allows the engine rpm to rise to the point where the turbocharger can be effective in generating more power. As the power comes in from the engine through the increased rpm, the drive can be lowered slightly to maximise the thrust and, once fully onto the plane, the shaft angle can be adjusted for maximum performance.

It takes experience to find the right setting for a trimmable surface drive and the best way is to try various settings in calm water, using the GPS to measure the speed. This will show you where the optimum setting lies on the trim indicator dial and you can use that as a reference when running in waves. It can look impressive running with the trim set high so that there is a big 'rooster tail' coming out of the stern, but this should only be seen when coming onto the plane and for normal efficient running the rooster tail should be quite low. As with stern drives, the drive shaft should be lowered slightly when in rough seas or when turning, and when manoeuvring in harbour it should be set low to get maximum propeller bite. It's also possible to experience porpoising with these drives in the same way as with outboards and stern drives, but trimming down slightly will usually cure this.

TRIMMABLE SURFACE DRIVES WHERE THE VERTICAL ANGLE OF THE DRIVE SHAFTS CAN BE ADJUSTED.

# 27 SETTING UP THE FLAPS

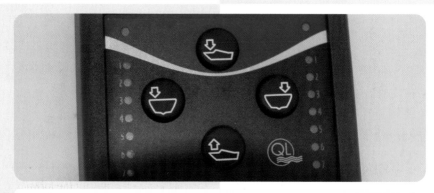

A FLAP CONTROL PANEL THAT SHOWS GRAPHICALLY THE EFFECT OF USING THE FLAPS.

Getting the right flap settings on a powerboat can make a tremendous difference to ride comfort and performance, so it's worth spending some time experimenting with settings. The flaps control both the fore and aft trim and the transverse trim, and on a fast boat getting the correct trim is important from both the ride comfort and performance point of view.

In calm conditions there should be no need to have any flap setting if the hull has been correctly designed in the first place. However, with different loadings, such as with full fuel or with a large number of people on board, it's worth lowering the flaps a little to see if this improves the performance. Check the speed on the GPS with the flaps on different settings. This should help you to get a feel for how the flaps affect the performance in calm water – but they are more useful in rougher seas.

In a head sea, introducing a measure of flap-down control will help to keep the bow down and should give a more level ride. Putting the flaps down will lower the bow and generate more spray, so

Flaps down – bow down

USING FLAPS TO TRIM DOWN THE BOW.

you have to find a balance. If you are on a passage on the same heading for some time, it's worth experimenting with the flap settings to find the best adjustment.

In following seas the flaps should be up in the horizontal position because you want the maximum lift at the bow to keep it up when the boat comes over the top of a wave. There should be no need for any flap setting in following seas, although if the waves are on the quarter there may be a need for one flap to be slightly down to balance the boat. In beam seas you will find that the boat will heel into the wind (as described in Heeling into the Wind, 28), so it's prudent to lower the windward flap to

counteract this and to get a level ride. At all times, when just one flap is lowered it will affect the steering because of the increased drag on that side and you will need to counteract this by a small steering offset.

When using flaps, the control switches or levers can be confusing at times. The logical system is for the port switch to control the port flap and for the forward end of the rocker switch to lower the flap. This forward end is usually labelled 'bow down', but some powerboat builders use a reverse logic and connect the port switch to the starboard flap on the basis that if the boat is heeling, you use the switch on the lower side to correct the heeling.

Whichever system is used on a particular boat, you will soon get used to it and every flap installation should include a dial to show just where the flaps are set at any time. Because of the importance of the flaps in balancing the boat, the switches should be located for is an easily accessible position.

Some boats are fitted with an automatic flap-control system that does the setting for you. While such a system can take some of the work out of controlling the boat, it will never give the subtle control of the flaps that can provide the best ride in adverse conditions.

↑ Port flap down –
port side up

Starboard flap down – ↑
starboard side up

THE EFFECT ON TRANSVERSE TRIM OF SINGLE-FLAP OPERATION.

# 28 HEELING INTO THE WIND

Drive a powerboat with the wind on the beam and you will notice that the boat heels into the wind. The stronger the wind, the more pronounced the effect, and with the underwater surfaces of the hull presenting a flatter surface to the water you can get a harsher ride. The deeper the vee, the more the angle of heel into the wind will be.

Even when running at speed, a powerboat will be deeper in the water at the stern than at the bow. When the wind is on the beam, the front of the hull will be more affected by the wind than the stern, and the wind pressure on this forward part will have the effect of pushing it downwind, while the stern has a firm grip on the water.

You will automatically adjust this tendency by applying a steering correction. In this way you will hold the boat on course, but as we saw in The Effect of Steering on Trim, 24, this steering correction will cause the boat to heel because of the side thrust generated and it is this that causes the boat to heel into the wind.

The solution is quite simple and the heeling can be corrected by dropping the windward flap. However, when the windward flap is lowered it will also create some added drag that will try to bring the boat round more into the wind at the bow. This will in effect cancel out the need for a steering correction, so everything here is working in your favour. It is then a question of finding the right position for the flap and the right balance of the boat for the conditions, but the correction should result in a smoother ride in rough seas.

The deeper the vee, the more sensitive the hull is likely to be and it may only take small adjustments and a light hand on the steering to find the right balance for the conditions.

Wind tends to blow the bow downwind

Steering angled to correct wind effect

Steering causes hull to heel

STEERING TO CORRECT THE WIND PRESSURE ON THE BOW CAN CAUSE THE HULL TO HEEL INTO THE WIND.

**THE SECONDARY CONTROLS**

By fitting a 2-speed gearbox between the engine and the propeller, the propulsion has more flexibility to meet different loading conditions and requirements.

By using the higher of the two available gear ratios, the engine can turn faster than the propeller, so the propulsion will develop a higher thrust. By switching to the lower of the two gear ratios, the engine will turn at a slower speed in relation to the propeller so the top speed can be extended. The added complication of the 2-speed gearbox can be justified by the greater propulsion flexibility that results. This can be particularly beneficial with a surface-piercing propeller where the propeller can be overloaded when it is operating in the fully submerged mode and when getting onto the plane.

The higher gear ratio of a 2-speed gearbox is engaged when operating at lower speeds and this is beneficial not only when the boat is climbing onto the plane but also when operating in rough seas. In rough seas you are more concerned with a quick throttle response and acceleration than a high top speed and the higher gear ratio will provide this. The higher gear will only be used in calmer seas when the boat is operating at or close to its top speed.

The difference between the two gear ratios would normally be around 1.2 to 1.3 so that the drive would be operating at 1:1 for high-speed work and would use the higher ratio of, say, 1:1.2 when good acceleration is required. This difference will make a significant difference to the performance, increasing the top speed by several knots and providing better acceleration and responsiveness at lower speeds.

Changing the gear ratio on these gearboxes is usually by an electric switch on the dashboard but gear changes should be made only when a high top speed is required or when the boat is slowing down. These gearboxes are not intended to vary the speed, as they are not designed for constant changing. In calmer conditions you would probably only change gear after the boat has come onto the plane and then change again when slowing down after a run. In rough conditions you would probably want to stay in higher gear ratio all the time because of the good acceleration.

A BOAT THAT WOULD BENEFIT FROM A 2-SPEED GEARBOX.

# 30 BALLASTING

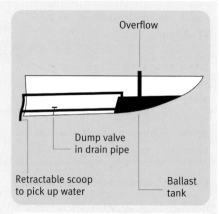

Overflow

Dump valve
in drain pipe

Retractable scoop
to pick up water

Ballast
tank

THE LAYOUT OF THE FILLING AND EMPTYING
ARRANGEMENTS FOR A BALLAST TANK.

Weight distribution is important on a powerboat in order to obtain the right level of fore and aft trim. If the designer has done his job correctly, the boat will be in balance for most conditions, but obviously he has to find a compromise that will work in most circumstances. To a certain degree the boat will balance itself to the changing speeds and sea conditions, and you can do a lot to help the balance by using the throttle, but the ability to shift weight on the boat can also help. As we saw in What Keeps your Boat Stable?, 11, the centre of gravity will normally stay in the same place, but if that can be moved in a fore and aft direction then the trim of the boat can be adjusted.

At sea, the only easily moveable weights are the crew. However, some high-performance powerboats have a bow ballast tank that allows weight to be added at the front of the boat; this can be a useful feature if you want to optimise performance in rough seas.

The main use of the bow ballast tank is to help keep the bow down when it lifts to a wave in head seas. In this way it does a similar job to flaps. Bow ballast tanks are a useful fitting if you can cope with the added complication and you want to maximise performance. There is also the added penalty of the extra weight of the system, but this can be justified when the performance of the boat in rough seas is the sole criterion.

The ballast tank can be filled and emptied with a cockpit control. Filling is usually achieved by lowering a scoop on the transom so that the forward motion of the boat forces water through pipes to the tank. An overflow pipe at deck level will indicate when the tank is full so that the scoop can be retracted. Emptying is through a drain valve on the tank so the system is kept relatively simple. You are unlikely to find bow ballast tanks fitted on a production powerboat on the basis that these boats are not driven close to the limits and so this complication isn't justified.

An alternative to using water ballast in this way is to use the fuel system. Fuel is normally carried in tanks located close to the centre of gravity so that the varying weight of the fuel doesn't affect the trim of the boat. If a secondary fuel tank is added near the bow and a transfer pump fitted, then fuel could be transferred forward to trim the boat without adding extra weight. Such a system has limitations as the fuel can't be used as ballast when it is getting low, but it can be a viable system to give extra trim flexibility.

A ballasting system could also be used to make life on board more comfortable in rough head seas and so could be justified on serious cruising boats. When operating in following seas the bow tank should be empty at all times so that there is maximum buoyancy in the bow to allow it to lift to the waves.

BALLASTING CAN HELP THIS RACE BOAT TO MAINTAIN A LEVEL TRIM IN HEAD SEAS.

# 31 BALANCING THE BOAT

The last few sections have shown that a number of factors can affect the performance of a powerboat. They have been dealt with individually, but when you are driving a boat in waves the distribution of the weight in the boat, the speed of the boat and above all the effect of the varying waves on the boat will tend to interact with one another. To compensate for these changes you have the various controls that we looked at in previous sections and you need to use them to find a balance between the individual effects.

This balancing will be largely a case of trial and error but if you find the right settings and balance in calm water first, you can take some of the variables out of the reckoning. This is particularly the case with the power trim, where you can find the optimum setting for different speeds in calm water runs. You may find the boat porpoising when operating close to full speed, and identify the need to introduce a small amount of flap control or vary theweight distribution to counteract this. Smaller boats will tend to be more sensitive to weight distribution than larger boats.

Waves are the main variable that you will need to compensate for and these come in all shapes and sizes, even in what looks like a regular wave train.

Here you have to find a balance using slow-acting controls such as the flaps and possibly the ballast tank, but it is the fast-acting throttles that give you the rapid control that you need to respond to waves.

Thus in a head sea you are likely to find a balance with the power trim partially in and the flaps partially down, using the throttle to lift or lower the bow in response to the shape and size of individual waves. Here you need to find the balance that keeps the bow down, while in following seas the situation will be reversed and you need to find a balance that keeps the bow up to prevent it from stuffing into the wave ahead.

Finding the required balance will be largely a case of experience in boat driving, combined with an understanding of the characteristics of the particular boat involved. Like many aspects of fast boat driving, there are few hard and fast rules and experimenting with small changes in the settings of the flaps and the power trim can often produce significant improvements. It may be possible to find a setting that is just right for the conditions, where the boat literally skims from wave top to wave top, but the size of the waves will have a significant bearing on what can be achieved in this respect – and remember, there will always be larger waves lurking out there, ready to upset your carefully achieved balance.

A BOAT THAT IS WELL BALANCED SHOULD BE A JOY TO DRIVE.

# 32 READING THE WAVES

THIS PICTURE SHOWS HOW THE WAVES CAN VARY IN SIZE AND SHAPE AND WHY IT IS IMPORTANT TO 'READ' THE WAVES.

Driving a powerboat in calm water is pretty straightforward once you have the trim correctly set. However, once you encounter waves, driving the boat becomes a more challenging experience.

In waves up to around half the length of the boat, it is usually possible to find a balance of the controls that allows you to ride at a fixed speed. Once the wavelength gets longer than the length of the boat, you need to 'read' the waves and make adjustments to continue making comfortable and hopefully rapid progress. Of course you can set the throttles at a lower speed so that a margin of safety is built in, but

you may get an uncomfotable ride because the boat can start riding up and down each wave rather than trying to bridge the gap between them. The alternative is to read the waves and adjust the throttle setting to match so that you help the boat through.

Reading the waves is a skill that needs developing and it is a prime requirement of driving a powerboat. Waves are very rarely even and in any wave train you will get high waves and low waves. The statistics suggest that one wave in about 20 will be twice the height of the average, and you should keep that in the back of your mind.

There is rarely just one wave train and two wave trains crossing can produce a pyramid type of wave rather than a long crest, and these can be harder to deal with because the wave peak tends to suddenly rear up close by. Then if you study the waves you will notice that they rarely have a long level crest but that there are peaks and troughs along the line of the crest. If you aim for the lower troughs you will get an easier ride.

While you will probably already be committed to the speed and attitude of the boat to the wave just ahead, this should be when you are concentrating on the wave after that. Waves will arrive rapidly in head seas because your boat speed is added to the wave speed, but you will have more time to read the waves in following seas. It's not so easy to see what the waves ahead are doing over the crest in following seas because you are approaching from upwind. In beam seas you will be focusing on the waves coming from upwind and trying to read what they are doing and how they will affect the boat.

Wave troughs are just as important as wave crests. Just as there are higher than average wave crests, so there are deeper troughs in between them and these can be more dangerous because you're not aware of them until you drop inside.

If you want to drive a powerboat with skill, then understanding the waves is vital. Time spent studying waves, how they form and how they behave is never time wasted.

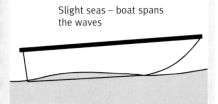

Slight seas – boat spans the waves

Moderate seas – boat starts to drop between each wave

Heavy seas – boat starts to contour the waves

AS WAVES GROW IN SIZE A FAST BOAT IS LESS ABLE TO ACCOMMODATE THE WAVE SHAPE.

Head seas present probably the biggest challenge to the driver of a powerboat because the waves arrive with only very short intervals between them. This means that the available reaction and response times are shortened. One obvious way to extend the time interval between wave crest encounters is to slow down and that would be the normal reaction, as the waves get higher.

Once you slow down, the boat will start to contour the waves, the bow rising and falling with the passing of each wave, and you can get a very uncomfortable ride. As the waves get larger you can find yourself slowing down to the point where the boat is virtually off the plane. In more extreme conditions this may be the only solution, but remember that as you slow down the bow of the boat drops and you are more likely to stuff

the bow into an oncoming wave. The tendency is to slow down again in what can become a vicious circle of slow progress.

The alternative is to start to drive the boat on the throttle to try to match the attitude of the boat to the waves. This requires concentration and a responsive boat. On a big heavy diesel boat this may not be a viable option, but on a smaller, faster powerboat, using the throttle can enable you to make good progress in adverse conditions.
The technique is to open the throttle as the boat approaches the wave to lift the bow. As the boat nears the crest, close

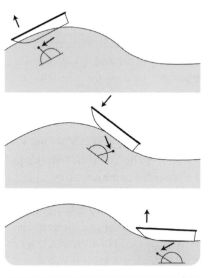

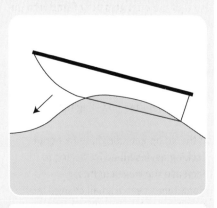

BOAT PUNCHING THROUGH A WAVE CREST, LEAVING THE BOW UNSUPPORTED

AN EXAGGERATED VIEW OF THE THROTTLE CONTROL WHEN OPERATING A FAST BOAT IN HEAD SEAS.

HEADING INTO THE WAVES IN A PLANING BOAT CAN BE A CHALLENGING EXPERIENCE.

the throttle to lower the bow so the boat cuts through the crest, then open it again to lift the bow for the next wave. The movements of the throttle should be quite small, just short bursts of power, so that the boat maintains a more or less steady speed and to a certain extent you are using the momentum of the boat to help bridge the gap between the wave crests.

In more moderate seas you can make fast progress by having the boat bridge the gap between the wave crests, but you will probably need the flaps down a touch to stop the bow lifting too much. You also need to keep an eye open for those larger than normal waves. You can use the steering to guide the boat through the lower sections of the wave crests, but only small amounts of helm

should be used to avoid the boat heeling over too much.

Driving in head seas requires a delicate hand on the throttle and steering and constant concentration. You need to take care not to close the throttle too far so that the boat gets out of step with the waves and the bow drops into a trough. It is natural to close the throttle when you see a big wave ahead and it can take courage to open rather than close it in this situation, to lift the bow over the wave rather than powering through it.

If the going gets tough, think about tacking as described in Tacking to increase the wavelength, 47. Sometimes even a small change in heading can improve the situation considerably.

# 34 WITH THE WAVES ON THE BEAM

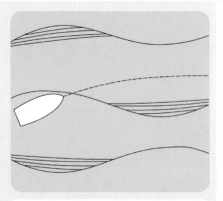

DODGING AREAS OF BREAKING WAVES IN A BEAM SEA.

If waves came in nice regular lines, driving with the wind and waves on the beam would be relatively easy and predictable. However, waves are rarely regular in this way and you will find that approaching waves will have highs and lows along the line of the crest, so you need to drive with a degree of caution and in particular to watch out for any waves that may have breaking crests. You should be able to make rapid progress when the wind is on the beam but, as always, you need to concentrate and be prepared for the unexpected.

The first thing to do when the wind and waves are on the beam is to lower the windward flap to keep the boat upright. This will improve the ride comfort by preventing the boat from heeling into the wind. When the waves are coming from the side, you will be using the steering rather than the throttle as the primary control, because in this situation the best solution can be to drive around the larger waves rather than use the throttle to negotiate your way over them.

The waves are obviously approaching from windward and there is the option of heading more upwind to pass through at a low point in the approaching crest or heading off downwind to find an easy route past. The downwind route appears to offer an easier path through the wave crests and is always going to be the more attractive choice. However, if you constantly take the downwind option, you can find yourself quite a way off course in a short time.

If it's important to stay on a particular course then you will need to make a conscious effort to take the upwind option at times. However, if just making fast progress is the important aspect then the downwind option is the one to go for. As always, if you want to make fast progress in beam seas, a high level of concentration is needed, and a clear view to windward in order to be able to watch the approaching waves.

In beam seas you need to focus on the waves some way ahead rather than those close by, because you need to take action at an earlier stage. It takes quite a bit of skill and judgement to anticipate just how the boat and the approaching wave will interact at a point some way ahead, but once you become comfortable with the conditions you should be able to make rapid progress. One factor in your favour when running with the wind on the beam is that the consequences of getting it wrong are unlikely to be serious, and even at the last minute you'll still be able to turn away downwind to escape from a close encounter with a breaking crest.

YOU NEED TO ANTICIPATE THE WAVES SOME WAY AHEAD IN BEAM SEAS. HERE THE BOAT SHOULD BE TURNING AWAY DOWNWIND TO AVOID THE BREAKING WAVE CREST.

# 35 COPING WITH FOLLOWING SEAS

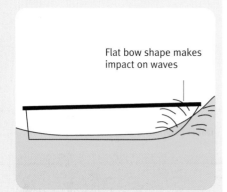

Flat bow shape makes impact on waves

IN A FOLLOWING SEA, A FLAT BOW SHAPE CAN IMPACT WITH THE WAVE IN FRONT.

When running a boat in following seas there is always the prospect of broaching. In a fast powerboat you are in a stronger position to negotiate the waves in a following sea because the boat will be travelling faster than the waves. This should enable you to dictate your position in relation to the waves, to put you in control and avoid the risk of broaching (see Broaching, 40).

Because you are travelling in the same direction as the waves, the period of encounter with the waves is much slower than in head seas. This gives you more time to get the speed correct to overtake a particular wave. However, in following seas it isn't always easy to assess the scale of a particular wave because you are approaching it from the back or the windward side. This is the more gentle side of the wave and the

boat will climb it only to face what can be quite a steep drop into the trough on the other side. The steeper side of a wave is always on the downwind side and this is what you will face as you come over the crest.

This is where you need delicate speed control. If the boat is going too slowly as it passes over the crest, the bow becomes unsupported, lacks momentum and can drop heavily into the trough. Too much speed and the boat will become airborne as it passes over the crest and drops into the trough. As always, much will depend on the size of the waves and with a wavelength up to around half the length of the boat there should be no problem. In larger waves, because boat and wave are travelling in the same direction there will be less momentum to help carry the boat through the crest at a level angle.

You do not want to be in a position where you have to close the throttle as you pass through the crest, as that will cause the bow to drop just when you want a level ride. The bow of the boat may stuff into the wave ahead, which in itself may not be serious but it can give a very wet and uncomfortable ride. Ideally you want to come over the crest and land on the next wave at about the same angle upwards as that wave. It is easy in principle but much harder to do

**DRIVING THE BOAT**

as you can't see what the situation is until you come over the crest.

In some waves, particularly in short steep seas, it can be very hard to find a comfortable speed and the best solution here is to alter course 20 or more degrees to space out the waves. In moderate following seas you should be able to find a comfortable running speed where the boat runs from crest to crest. In a following sea, you want the flaps up (except if you need them for balancing the transverse trim), the drive trimmed out to keep the bow up, and any ballast tanks forward should be empty.

THE SORT OF BREAKING WAVE CREST YOU NEED TO DRIVE AWAY FROM IN A FOLLOWING SEA.

# 36 EXPECT THE UNEXPECTED

When driving a powerboat you must always expect the unexpected. Even in calm conditions you should not take anything for granted. Concentration is needed at all times because the sea is constantly changing and circumstances can change without warning.

Even on a calm day you could suddenly meet the wash of a passing vessel, catching you unawares. Take particular care with fast ferries, with their 2m (6ft) wash waves. Container and passenger ships also create significant wash and you are likely to feel the effects up to 1.6km (1 mile) away.

When wind is generating significant waves, the wash of passing vessels may be partially hidden, only to reveal itself as larger than normal waves. These will be in addition to the larger than average waves found in any wave train. Conditions can also change when passing around headlands or entering areas with a stronger tidal flow. Around headlands you can expect to find stronger tides and stronger winds, so conditions here could be temporarily worse and in areas of strong tides the difference between one direction of flow and another can be quite significant – enough to make getting home a challenging task.

Wind against tide conditions produce the short, steep seas that are not friendly to a fast powerboat. As the driver, you can see what is happening but your passengers will not. Sudden changes in speed, sudden turns and unexpected impacts with waves can catch them out and even throw them about the boat. As the driver you have a responsibility towards your passengers and it is important to shout warnings so that they can prepare for sudden movements. The unexpected can and does happen at sea quite frequently and in a fast boat this means being ready for all eventualities.

BREAKING SEAS AROUND A HEADLAND, CAUSED BY THE WIND RUNNING AGAINST THE TIDE, CAN CREATE AN UNEXPECTED DETERIORATION IN CONDITIONS.

DRIVING THE BOAT

Porpoising is experienced on powerboats where the bow goes up and down at speed. It seems to occur without reason so you feel a bit out of control, which can be disconcerting when running at 40 knots or more. You are more likely to experience porpoising in calm conditions than when operating in waves and it tends to occur at higher rather than lower speeds.

The basic problem behind porpoising is that there is too little of the hull in the water to enable it to find a point of balance. One minute the bow is too low and the point of lift moves forward, lifting the bow, and the next minute the bow is too high with the point of lift too far aft. The balance can also be affected by weight distribution in the boat. If weight is added towards the stern, this affects the trim and can cause the boat to porpoise.

There are various ways to cure the problem. If you think it might be caused by extra weight from passangers in the stern, either move them forward or lower the flaps slightly to generate more lift at the stern. Either way, the bow will be lowered to give a longer area of the hull in the water so that the fore and aft balance is not so critical.

Porpoising may start as you trim the drive out, which will tend to lift the bow and reduce the length of the hull in the water. If this does occur just bring the drive in slightly. You may need to use both flaps and power trim but that would suggest that the boat is out of balance and may need a more fundamental change of trim by shifting weight within the hull.

The reason you are unlikely to find the boat porpoising in rough water is that encounters with waves will vary the length of the hull that is in the water and help to stabilise it. Any tendency for the hull to porpoise will thus be cancelled out by the wave encounters before it can become apparent.

THE TYPE OF SMALL, FAST BOAT WHERE YOU COULD EXPERIENCE PORPOISING BECAUSE ONLY A SMALL PART OF THE HULL IS IN THE WATER.

# 38 DRIVING ON THE EDGE

CHALLENGING CONDITIONS THAT DEMAND INTENSE CONCENTRATION AND SKILL.

One of the problems with driving a fast powerboat is that you don't know where the limits of performance are until you find them. Natural caution should prevent you from getting anywhere near the limits as you will usually frighten yourself long before you near the point of disaster. One of the safe features of modern powerboats is that the boat is usually far stronger than its crew, so even if you do make a mistake it is likely to be the crew that will suffer first rather than the boat and you will tend to ease up on the speed.

However, as you develop your skills you

**COPING WITH EXTREMES**

will want to push it closer and closer to the limits. There can be tremendous pleasure in driving a boat when you know that you have set up the trim to its optimum and you can push the throttles to the stops and revel in the thrill of driving a boat close to its limits for the conditions. If you want a reason for doing this, then offshore powerboat racing is probably the sport for you because it allows you to see if what you consider to be the limits are the same as those for other people.

Otherwise, if you feel the need to drive on the edge then perhaps you should do it when you are alone in the boat. You are more likely to learn from your mistakes without having someone looking over your shoulder and it is better to frighten only yourself rather than your passengers.

The edge of performance for a powerboat will vary with the prevailing conditions and full performance may only be possible in benign conditions. Once you have to start negotiating waves, your level of skill and

concentration will largely determine performance. This is where small adjustments to the trim can produce benefits and where your hand on the throttle will control not only the speed of the boat but also its performance in waves.

Fine-tuning of performance is something you can only learn from experience. There will always be a temptation to pull the throttle back when you feel that you have overdone things, but (as we have seen in previous chapters) in that situation closing the throttle can make things worse because the bow will drop. Although there are no hard and fast rules and every situation must be taken on its merits, opening the throttle when you feel you have overdone things can be a better solution than closing it. It only takes a quick burst to lift the bow and that may be enough to get you out of trouble, but it takes a bit of courage to overcome the natural instinct to close the throttle when things get out of hand, particularly when you are driving on the edge.

# 39 SPINNING OUT

THIS BOAT IS CLOSE TO SPIN-OUT WITH THE BOW FAIRLY DEEP AND THE STERN GETTING LIGHT.

Spinning out in a powerboat is a dramatic experience. It involves the boat turning end for end very rapidly and it can result in the crew being injured or thrown out of the boat. There are several reasons that a powerboat might spin out and understanding the causes can help to prevent it occurring.

The most likely cause of a spin-out is when turning a little too sharply. This is something that happens in offshore racing and it occurs when the boat is going too fast when it enters the turn and there is a natural instinct to close the throttle. Closing the throttle at this point causes the bow to drop, digging into the water where it now acts as a fulcrum around which the boat will spin. With most of the weight of a powerboat concentrated aft, the spin-out will be fast and uncontrollable once it starts. The way to prevent this type of spin-out is to enter a turn slowly and then speed up on leaving it. A wide approach will also help, but in racing you want to take

**COPING WITH EXTREMES**

the shortest route so drivers tend to push their luck with a tight turn.

Another type of spin-out can occur when the boat is travelling fast enough in waves for it to become airborne. If the boat is not properly balanced and comes down bow first, then again the bow can act as a fulcrum and, with the weight of the machinery aft, this can make the stern try to overtake the bow and the boat then spins. This can happen if the throttle is closed at the wrong moment when the boat is coming over a wave. A spin-out can also happen if the steering is over to one side or the other when the boat lands after becoming airborne.

A third cause of spinning out can be on a boat with an outboard or stern-drive propulsion where there is a direct feedback from the steering. Letting go of the wheel for any reason, even momentarily, will cause the helm to spin rapidly to the hard-over position under the propeller side torque and this can cause the boat to spin out unless it is controlled quickly. This possibility can be reduced if the torque tab is set correctly (as shown in Setting up outboards, 14) and it can be eliminated by using zero-torque steering.

Spinning out is most likely to occur when a powerful boat is being driven hard in waves when racing. A boat with

powerful and heavy engines in comparison to the overall weight of the boat will also be more prone to spinning out. A more cautious speed should prevent the boat approaching the spin-out point but there will be no warning of an impending spin-out so it is difficult to know where the limit lies. While it won't prevent a spin-out, having the driver wear a 'kill cord' to cut the engine will at least reduce the consequences.

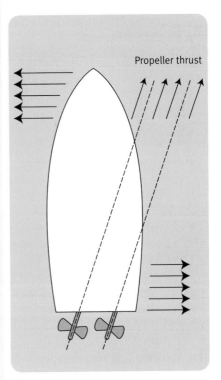

Propeller thrust

THE MECHANICS OF ONE TYPE OF SPIN-OUT, WHERE THE PROPELLER THRUST IS OFF-CENTRE AND HAS NOTHING TO REACT AGAINST WHEN THE HULL IS AIRBORNE.

A BOAT BEING OVERTAKEN BY A BREAKING WAVE NEEDS THE THROTTLES OPENED TO DRIVE AWAY FROM THE WAVE CREST.

Broaching is a form of spinning out but only occurs in following seas and tends to happen at much slower speeds than those normally used by powerboats. It occurs when a boat is on the downwind slope of a following wave where the bow of the boat is most likely to be immersed in the trough or into the back of the next wave in front. In this position the breaking crest of the wave coming up behind can be running down the downwind slope of the wave and impact on the boat, exerting the force that will spin the boat.

In this situation it is the bow of the boat that again acts as a fulcrum about which the flowing water will

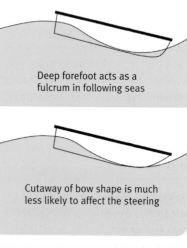

Deep forefoot acts as a fulcrum in following seas

Cutaway of bow shape is much less likely to affect the steering

THE EFFECT OF BOW SHAPE ON A BOAT'S BEHAVIOUR IN A FOLLOWING SEA.

force the boat to turn. In broaching, the bow is immersed in the next wave so it could be deeper in the water than the stern, allowing the boat to spin. The potential danger of this situation comes from the fact that with the boat turned beam on to the breaking wave crest in the spin, it will be rolled over by the advancing water.

Broaching shouldn't be a major problem facing a fast powerboat because the boat has the speed to drive itself out of the situation. It only takes a blip on the throttle to accelerate away from the breaking crest and this will also help to lift the bow so that the boat quickly moves out of potential danger. In the open sea, waves may travel at up to 25 knots, but in the shallow inshore waters and harbour entrances where broaching is more likely to occur, waves may be travelling at half that speed. Any planing powerboat will almost certainly have the speed to travel faster than the waves so it is possible for the driver to dictate the position of the boat in relation to the waves and to drive the boat out of trouble.

However, a cautious driver might be tempted to close the throttle when he sees a situation like this developing, and this slowing of the boat could be just the action that takes the boat into

danger of broaching. It does require a sensitive hand on the throttle when driving in following seas, because you want to be overtaking the waves but at the same time you don't want to push the bow too hard into the wave in front until the bow has lifted. If you're driving the boat through a harbour entrance where there is shallow water, an onshore wind, and waves are likely to be breaking, it pays to keep a careful watch on the waves astern as well as those ahead.

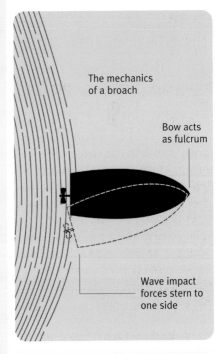

The mechanics of a broach

Bow acts as fulcrum

Wave impact forces stern to one side

THE BOW CAN ACT AS A FULCRUM WHEN THE BOAT IS BEING OVERTAKEN BY A BREAKING WAVE.

# 41 NIGHT DRIVING

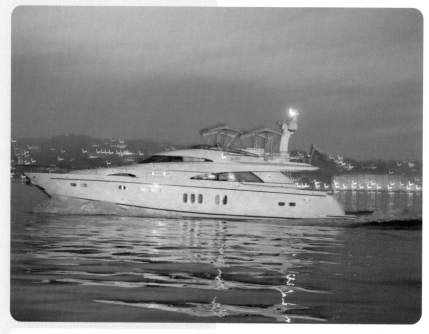

NIGHT-RUNNING IN CALM SEAS IS EASY BUT COPING WITH WAVES AT NIGHT REQUIRES MUCH MORE CAUTION.

Driving a powerboat in the dark is a challenging experience. After reading this book, you will be aware of how much you depend on seeing what is going on around the boat to ensure good and safe driving. If you take away the ability to see the waves at night, the situation becomes much more critical – and a much more cautious approach is required.

In calm conditions you should be able to maintain a reasonable speed at night but you do need to be more conscious of the possibility of the wash from passing ships creating unexpected waves. You should be able to see the lights of any shipping that might cause wash waves, and it pays to give considerable attention to them and to work out their headings so that you can anticipate when these waves might arrive.

When running in waves at night you need to moderate the speed considerably, but not too much. If you want to make reasonable progress then you need to keep the boat on the plane and that will probably mean a speed of at least 20 knots. If the boat runs comfortably at the chosen speed, that's fine, as long as you feel confident that you have a margin to cope with larger waves when they come along. In moderate seas you should be able to find a speed that works for the conditions, but slowing down too much will start the boat contouring the waves and that can lead to a quite uncomfortable motion. If you have to slow down because of the conditions, then slow down considerably to perhaps 7 or 8 knots.

A big heavy boat is going to be more comfortable when running at night than a lightweight boat, because it will be less affected by the waves. The weight of the boat will tend to give it a more level and comfortable ride. At night you will have to resort more to feeling the waves rather than seeing them, so the motion of the boat will give a good indication of what is going on.

It isn't just driving the boat at night that can be more difficult. Navigating at night can also be tricky because now you are relying on flashing navigation lights rather than landmarks and other features to see where you are. It can pay to keep the boat on autopilot steering in order to maintain a steady course and this will give more time to focus on the navigation and the throttling of the boat. The steady course should give a more comfortable ride but it will also mean that flashing lights will reappear on much the same bearing each time they show, which makes it easier to locate them as they pass.

With hand steering it's easy to wander off course by 20 degrees or more because you cannot give your full attention to the compass. In this situation, flashing lights are likely to appear to wander around the horizon, making them difficult to see. Another point to note at night is that it's very hard to judge distances from a quick flashing light and you can find yourself getting very close without realising it.

RUNNING ON AUTOPILOT AT NIGHT CAN TAKE A LOT OF THE STRESS OUT OF THE SITUATION.

# 42 FOG DRIVING

WHEN APPROACHING A FOG BANK, IT IS TIME TO SLOW DOWN.

Poor visibility can have a considerable impact on the way you drive a powerboat. The fog would have to be really thick to affect your ability to read the waves, so the actual driving of the boat is not an issue. The main concern is the increased risk of collision with other vessels. The collision regulations require you to reduce speed in fog, but what is meant by reduced speed is not defined. In reality a safe reduced speed would be one where, when you sight another vessel, you have time to stop before a collision occurs.

This doesn't mean you can stop within the range of the visibility because another vessel will also be moving, so you will meet somewhere in the middle of the range of visibility. To ensure a safe speed, you need to be able to stop within half the range of visibility.

Working out the range of visibility in fog is difficult and you will only get a good idea when you sight a fixed object such as a buoy. By using the GPS, you can work out how far away you are from the buoy when it is sighted and thus get an idea of the range of visibility. If you are leaving harbour in poor visibility you can get a range measurement as you leave, but in either case remember that the range of visibility can change significantly over a short period of time so any measurement you make may not be valid for long.

You will have to estimate what the range of visibility is as you go along using any measurements you can make from a buoy or other fixed object. Then you need to know the stopping distance of your boat which you can measure quite easily with GPS readings. On a planing powerboat your stopping distance will be quite short, probably less than 100m (330ft), but you have to remember that some electronic diesel engines won't allow you to switch directly from ahead to astern gear and they have a built-in time delay to prevent possible damage to the gearbox.

Even so, the stopping distance is likely to be quite short, so a moderate speed in fog could be something in the order of 20 knots provided that you are keeping a good lookout. On a practical level the range of visibility is only as good as when you actually see the other vessel and that could occur some way inside the visual range. As with night driving, running the boat on autopilot can relieve you of the pressure of having to steer and give you more time for a lookout. Taking avoiding action by steering out of trouble is a better alternative to stopping and you need to

know where the standby button is on the autopilot so you can disconnect it quickly.

In fog you need to maintain a high level of concentration at all times and if you are unfortunate enough to have the combination of fog and darkness then perhaps this is the time to seek harbour or a safe anchorage until things clear.

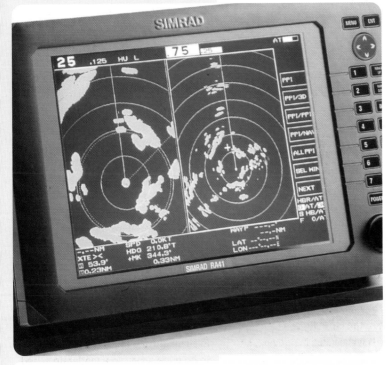

A DUAL RADAR DISPLAY SHOWING TWO DIFFERENT RANGE SCALES, WHICH CAN BE A GREAT HELP IN FOG.

# 43 COMING OFF THE PLANE

When a powerboat comes off the plane handling becomes totally different. You would probably only normally be operating off the plane when you are in harbour in calm conditions, where you can feel quite comfortable with the different handling characteristics. When you are out at sea driving in waves and you come down off the plane, you will be faced with a different set of circumstances that can be quite disconcerting.

There are two situations where you might come off the plane at sea. One is where the conditions are deteriorating and the boat is starting to slam heavily in the waves. Here you will want to reduce the speed to make things more comfortable, and as conditions deteriorate, you can find yourself easing the speed to the point where the boat comes off the plane. The other situation is where you are using the throttle to control the attitude and speed of the boat, usually in head seas, and you inadvertently pull the throttle back too far and the boat comes off the plane.

There are obviously going to be some sea conditions where you will have to operate at slow displacement speeds to reduce the stresses on the boat and the crew. This will usually be when operating in head seas when waves become short and steep. With the bow much lower

than when operating at planing speed, the stress of the boat may be relieved – but there can be a risk of shipping green water over the bow. If you find yourself in this situation, then an alteration of course may provide a solution and enable you to get the boat back onto the plane or at least give you a more comfortable and less stressful ride.

Inadvertently closing the throttle too far when driving the boat in waves can happen when heading in any direction. It will usually occur when you have throttle and gear controls combined in one lever and the range of throttle movement is quite limited. With some high-speed diesels, the power only comes in towards the top end of the engine operating speed. If you pull the throttle lever back too far in an attempt to reduce speed, you can find the boat coming off the plane; there isn't the quick response required to get the boat back onto the plane before it drops right off. This can lead to some uncomfortable moments because planing powerboats don't tend to operate comfortably at low speeds in waves and you won't feel that you have a good control over the situation.

It is a natural reaction to pull the throttle back quickly if you don't like what you see ahead, but in many cases you will get a better response by leaving the throttle alone or even possibly opening it for a short burst. It takes skill and experience to do this but it is a tactic that is used in racing. You have to remember that any short burst of throttle isn't likely to have much, if any, effect on the speed of the boat, but it can have a marked effect on the trim – a very important consideration when operating in waves. If you find yourself out in the sort of conditions where the driving is starting to become critical in this way, then it's time that you started to look for shelter or at least find a course where the ride is less stressful and you can run with the boat still on the plane.

A BOAT RUNNING OFF OR NEARLY OFF THE PLANE WILL HAVE A SLOW RESPONSE TO CHANGING CONDITIONS.

When you are driving a powerboat, you have your hands full with the controls and keeping a lookout. Chartwork can take second place and you need to simplify things as much as possible to make the navigation straightforward. It can be difficult, if not impossible, to do chartwork when under way and it can often be hard to read the detail on the chart. This applies to both paper and electronic charts, but you can do a great deal here to fine-tune the charts to your requirements.

Paper charts have a huge amount of information on them and there is so much detail that you often have to study them closely to see what is shown. Spread out on a table when you are planning the route it all looks easy, but in the confines of a powerboat chart table (if you have one) and when the boat is moving about at sea, the detail is rarely as clear as you would like it to be. The different colours for soundings can help to give you a general picture, but features such as isolated dangers and even buoys may not be clear when you are navigating at speed.

Customising the chart can be a good idea. Obviously you will draw in the routes to be followed and these can be identified with the courses and distances marked on them. A longer course could be marked every 8km (5 miles) or so, so that you can do a mental calculation about progress along that leg.

Buoys and other marks can be highlighted by circling them, and if you are navigating at night then write down the characteristics of the lights so that you don't need to look at the small print on the chart. Similarly, conspicuous objects – particularly if they are close to the heading you will be steering – are a good feature to identify, and isolated dangers and shoals should also be highlighted. In this way you have adapted the chart into a display tailored to your particular requirements. You might want to highlight the inshore depths in places where you could be passing close to shallow water.

Highlighting and making notes on the chart can be done in pencil for a one-off route that you will want to erase after it has been used, but if you use the area frequently you can make more permanent changes by using highlighter pens and different colours for buoys and lights. It can also be a good idea to mark a variety of possible courses on the chart so that you have options readily available when you are at sea, and to make a note of the tide times in pencil – then you have virtually all the navigation information you need on one chart.

The electronic chart is now widely used for powerboat navigation because it does most of the hard work automatically. Electronic charts suffer from the same problems as the paper chart in showing too much detail on a small-sized screen, but here you are limited in what you can do to customise the chart. The courses and distances to the next waypoint are shown, but unfortunately, there's no way that you can highlight buoys or other features that you might be passing close to. On most systems you can put the cursor on a feature and a small panel will show the details, such as the light characteristics of a buoy.

Some systems have a de-clutter control that can remove superfluous information, while others have a menu that allows for some detail to be removed, but there is no facility for magnifying and highlighting the significant features that are important, so you always need to give electronic charts a detailed scrutiny to ensure that you are seeing all the relevant information.

THIS IS THE WAY RACE BOAT NAVIGATORS FINE-TUNE THEIR CHARTS TO MEET THEIR HIGH SPEED REQUIREMENTS.

**NAVIGATION PREPARATION**

PART OF YOUR NAVIGATION PREPARATION CAN INCLUDE HIGHLIGHTING NAVIGATION FEATURES SUCH AS THIS BEACON AND THE DISTANT RADIO MAST.

The message in Before you Leave, 5, was that it's much easier to do things when the boat is steady and stable in harbour than when out at sea. This applies particularly to navigation and while, of course, you will be doing the actual navigation as you go along, setting everything up before you leave is essential on a powerboat.

As we saw in Fine-tuning the Chart, 44, it can be difficult, if not impossible, to write or draw lines on a chart when the boat is in motion, so if you are using paper charts and visual navigation, all the required courses should be marked on the chart. Measure and note the distances between waypoints so that you can assess the time it will take between the points. Mark and possibly highlight any buoys or other navigation marks located on or near your route, and indicate what the tide is doing and when the tidal flow will change.

You should go through much the same process if you are using electronic navigation. Many electronic screens are quite small, so trying to work out the detail can be difficult if the boat is moving about in waves. If you have planned and plotted all your courses and routes beforehand, you can have confidence that the courses you marked on the electronic chart will keep you out of danger. The actual navigation work will mainly be monitoring the track and adjusting the courses being steered so that you follow your desired track.

Unfortunately, you cannot tailor the electronic chart in the way that you can a paper chart, so in practice you will tend to use a combination of visual and electronic navigation in most situations when you are within sight of land. This double preparation may sound like overkill, but if you generally navigate in the same area the marked-up paper chart can be used over and over again. The benefits of preparing the two systems side by side are that you're less likely to miss any significant features and, more importantly, you will have a back-up system ready to go should the electronic system fail.

Part of the preparation work should be in setting up the electronic chart to meet your navigation requirements. The sub-menus of the electronic systems have a wide selection of options regarding what is actually displayed, allowing you to remove a lot of superfluous information from the display to make it easier to interpret – but take care that you don't remove essential navigation items.

PASSING A BUOY CAN GIVE A REASSURING VISUAL CHECK ON THE NAVIGATION.

The electronic chart is a tremendous help in navigating a powerboat as it does most of the navigation work for you. However, it is not good practice to rely solely on electronics and visual navigation should be part of your navigation repertoire. On a powerboat you cannot use the established techniques of compass bearings and calculation to establish your position, but there are enough visual clues out there to give you a reasonable idea of where you are and where you are going. Awareness of your surroundings and relating what you see to what is shown on the chart can be a useful check even if you are using GPS as your primary means of navigation. Practising and exercising your visual navigation skills will also reduce the amount of panic you feel if you get some form of electronic failure.

Navigation buoys will be your main clue for visual navigation because they are laid in position for that specific purpose. However, a study of the paper chart will give you a very good idea of what else you might expect to see and what features might prove useful.

Out in the open sea, the only positional clues you are likely to get are from soundings. A deeper or a relatively shallow area can often indicate where you cannot be as much as where you are – which can be just as important.

Closer to the land there will be many clues to indicate your position – for example, two identifiable marks on the shore in line or nearly in line will give

you a position line and you must be somewhere along it.

It can be useful to practise judging distances at sea because they can help to fix a position. Judging how far you are off a headland can help to avoid off-lying dangers, particularly when used in conjunction with soundings. Visual navigation is a bit like detective work, and it is by combining some or all of these clues that you can often get a pretty good idea of where you are.

PASSING A BUOY NOT ONLY FIXES YOUR POSITION BUT CAN INDICATE WHAT THE TIDE IS DOING.

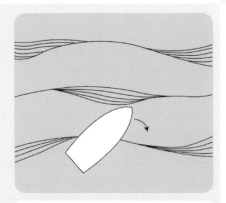

TACKING ACROSS THE WAVES CAN IMPROVE THE RIDE BUT BREAKING WAVES ON THE BOW CAN CAUSE THE BOAT TO SWING BEAM-ON UNLESS THERE IS A GOOD STEERAGE WAY.

Sailboats don't have a choice when they are heading into the wind. They have to tack across the wind because they cannot sail directly into it. Powerboats have an unlimited choice of the direction in which they can head, but sometimes it can pay a powerboat to tack across the wind in order to improve the ride.

In this book there are many references to the way a powerboat ride can become increasingly difficult when heading into the waves and when the weather is deteriorating. Wind against tide conditions can be particularly difficult to cope with, as the wavelength is so short that the boat cannot recover between one wave and the next. It's not just head seas that can make life difficult – you can have similar problems in following seas when the waves are short and steep.

In these situations it can pay to engage sailboat techniques and use tacking to improve things. As soon as you start going at an angle to the sea, you increase the wavelength because there is a longer distance between the wave crests when they are crossed at an angle. Any increase in the wavelength is going to be beneficial and, while the route might be longer, tacking opens up the possibility of running at a higher speed to complete the journey. Tacking could mean the difference between staying on the plane and having to come off the plane in difficult head seas, but in addition to being able to run at a better speed there is also the prospect of a more comfortable ride.

In following seas, tacking should be used with a degree of caution. Going over a following wave at an angle can expose you to breaking crests on your quarter, so you need to drive looking over your shoulder so see what is coming up astern. A breaking crest could loom up quite close alongside you where the wash of your boat meets an already unstable wave crest, and you may need to turn away and head directly downwind to get away. The benefits of tacking may not be so great in following seas as they are in head seas, but they can be an option worth trying.

# TACKING TO INCREASE THE WAVELENGTH

Even in beam seas tacking can be an option, and one of the techniques described in With the waves on the beam, 34, is to turn off slightly downwind to escape from any breaking crests or high waves that loom up alongside. Here you will probably only have to turn away 10 or 20 degrees to get a better ride and this is something to remember in any attempt to use tacking techniques in a powerboat. Unlike a sailboat, you are not restricted by the wind direction in how much or how little you alter course. You can turn just the amount that improves the ride and it is worth experimenting with different course angles to find the best result.

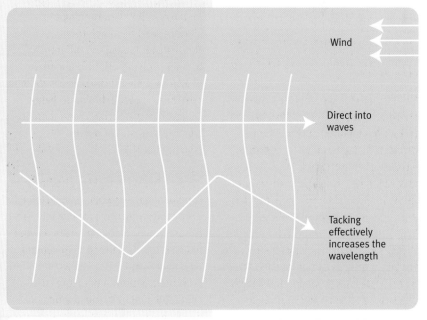

Wind

Direct into waves

Tacking effectively increases the wavelength

TACKING EFFECTIVELY INCREASES THE WAVELENGTH.

# 48 TAKING THE LONGER ROUTE

Driving in coastal waters – where most smaller craft operate – can open up the possibilites of useful tactics in poor weather but it can also limit your options. The limitations come from the fact that the land, or perhaps shallow water, will prevent you heading in certain directions or having access to certain areas. The benefits can come from the possibility of using the land to gain some shelter. When conditions are poor it can often pay to take a longer route in order to find shelter and than be able to maintain a better speed.

Running under the shelter of the land may allow you to complete a passage when the conditions further out at sea are untenable. However, be aware of any forecast suggesting that the wind direction may change and leave you exposed. Also while the forecast may show wind coming off the land, the local winds will often run along the coastline, especially in narrow channels, where the wind will normally blow either up or down the channel but rarely across it.

You have very few options available if you have to round a headland. There are no short cuts or alternative routes, but in the sections between you can improve your speed and comfort, especially when the wind is coming from ahead.

DRIVING IN COASTAL WATERS CAN LIMIT YOUR OPTIONS.

As we saw in Tacking to increase the wavelength, 47, if you angle the course across the waves rather than directly into them then you should get an improved ride. Heading into the bays between headlands rather than directly across the bay will put the wind on the bow and this should give you an immediate improvement in ride comfort. Once you have headed into the bay, you will be closing on land and the plan then should be to head along

**TACTICS AND NAVIGATION**

the coast on the inside of the bay. This may bring the wind back right ahead, but as you approach the next headland you will be running steadily into the more sheltered waters that are protected by it. Even when rounding it you can often find better sea conditions close inshore where the tides are weaker.

The chances are that by taking the longer route you will not only get a more comfortable ride but you should also be able to maintain a higher speed. Before you adopt this tactic you need to check the chart carefully to make sure that there are no shoals and isolated rocks that could impede your progress.

Tides are likely to have some effect on the sea conditions, your progress and tactics. You will almost certainly find less tide close inshore, which could lead to improved conditions and a faster passage, and you need to take all these things into consideration when plotting your inshore tactics.

BY TAKING THE LONGER ROUTE YOU CAN GET A MORE COMFORTABLE RIDE AND MAINTAIN A HIGHER SPEED.

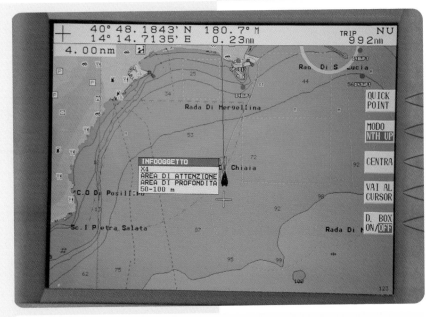

THE HEADING MARKER ON THE ELECTRONIC CHART SHOWS YOU WHERE YOU ARE GOING.

The use of electronics has revolutionised the way fast boats are navigated. Before electronics, the navigator would spend much of his time trying to work out the position of the boat. Now, the GPS gives you constant positional information with a high degree of accuracy. This means you can now focus on where the boat is going rather than trying to work out where it is. This is the key to fast-boat navigation and the electronic chart can do most of the work for you.

If you have done the preparation work (as detailed in Visual navigation, 46),

you should have all the desired waypoints and courses marked on the electronic chart. Now all you have to do is get the boat to follow the desired track. On many systems, you can link the autopilot into the electronic chart and the boat will automatically follow the desired track. This is not a good idea because it leaves the electronics in control and you won't be monitoring progress as closely as you should. By all means set the autopilot up to steer the boat so that you can focus on navigation and on collision avoidance, but do the course alterations at waypoints, and any